WHO'S BURIED WHERE IN LEICESTERSHIRE

WHO'S BURIED WHERE IN LEICESTERSHIRE

by
Joyce Lee

edited by
Jon Dean

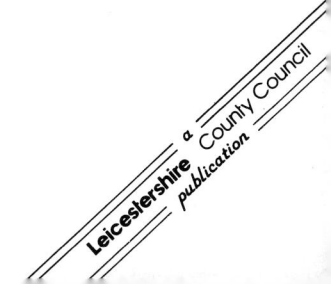

Leicestershire Libraries & Information Service

a Leicestershire County Council publication

© Joyce M Lee 1991

Published 1991.
Leicestershire Libraries and informationService.
Thames Tower, 99 Burleys Way, Leicester. LE1 3TZ.

All rights reserved. No part of this publication may be photocopied, recorded or otherwise reproduced, stored in a retrieval system or transmitted in any form or by any electronic or mechanical means without prior permission of the copyright owner.

ISBN 085 022 291 5
Cover Design by Sue Morris
Printed by Automedia, Loughborough.

CONTENTS

Acknowledgements	6
Introduction	7
1. Unusual tombs and monuments	9
2. Scientists, engineers and doctors	36
3. Artists and musicians	59
4. Local characters	69
5. Industrialists, benefactors and reformers	80
6. Celebrities, heroes and sporting personalities	101
7. Villains and victims	118
8. Accidents and misfortunes	132
9. Sovereigns, courtiers and politicians	141
10. Trades and occupations	167
11. Connections	179
A guide to sources	188
Select bibliography	197
Gazetteer	200
Index to people	209

Acknowledgements

I am indebted to Jon Dean who not only edited the text, but also carried out much of the field work with me and gave his help and support throughout.

Claire Wallin.

I should also like to thank the following for their help:

Ashby-de-la-Zouch Town Council, Blaby District Council, David Bodicoat (Quorn), N. H. Bovey (Laughton), Kathleen Bray (Bitteswell), Charnwood Borough Council, Jean Clarke (Coston), Terry Cocks (Knighton), Mrs F. E. Davies (Barrow-upon-Soar), Hilda Davis (Leicestershire Family History Society), John Deave (Stathern), R. Dempsey (H. M. Prison Leicester), S. S. East (Little Bowden), Marian Elliott (Birstall), Eileen Grewcock (Swepstone), Leslie Hales (Leicestershire Family History Society), Simon Harrington, Lady Henig, Hinckley and Bosworth Borough Council, Brother Jonathan (Mount St. Bernard Abbey), June King (Rothley), Pam Knowles (Barrow-upon-Soar), J. W. Lawrance (Earl Shilton), Mr Lowe (Loughborough and District Archaeological Society), Harborough District Council, Anne P. Marston (Gaddesby), Melton Borough Council, C. F. W. Nickolls (Saxelbye), North West Leicestershire District Council, Oadby and Wigston Borough Council, John Porter (Leicester City Council), Ken Round (Ashby-de-la-Zouch), Val Sargeant, Shirley Scott (Birstall), Margaret Shaw (Leicestershire Family History Society), Kathleen Shepherd (Sutton Cheney), Rosemary Spoor (Laughton), Mrs D. A. Staveley (The Belvoir Estate), Sue Templeman (Quorn), H. Thompson (Lockington), W. H. Topley (Burrough-on-the-Hill), Miss J. Turner (Belton-in-Rutland), Barbara Webb (Twyford), Dawn Whatton (Leicester City Council).

Friends and colleagues in Leicestershire Libraries and Information Service especially Jane Hipwell and the Publications and Publicity Team, Aubrey Stevenson, Mike Raftery and Dorothy Bamford.

Staff at Leicestershire Record Office and the Leicester Mercury Library.

The Leicester Mercury, Leicestershire Museums Arts and Records Service, the National Army Museum, the National Portrait Gallery and Oxford University Press for permission to reproduce the illustrations and quotations as indicated.

Mary Clark who suggested the original idea for the book.

Also many more individuals including the incumbents, officials and numerous keyholders of Leicestershire's churches whose help was invaluable.

Introduction

Interest in churchyards, burial grounds and cemeteries has greatly increased over the last few decades particularly amongst the growing numbers of family history researchers and local historians. Many others including photographers, biographers and tourists share a fascination for the subject, with common interests in finding out who's buried where, whether any monument exists, and discovering something about the person concerned.

Although various guides have been published to England's more famous graves and notable cemeteries, there has been little specifically for Leicestershire. "Who's Buried Where in Leicestershire" is intended to help fill this gap. Firstly it is a guide to people of renown or historical interest whose tombs are in Leicestershire. As well as this it includes a selection of the county's more unusual and eccentric monuments. Both the historic counties of Leicestershire and Rutland are covered, the Gazetteer showing at a glance who is associated with each place.

Almost 200 people are included ranging from ancient British rulers to twentieth century celebrities. Notable figures include England's first orthopaedist, the father of the modern travel industry, a pioneer of social research, and the first Englishman known to have visited Central Asia. Amongst the many others of interest are the local composer who introduced Beethoven's music into England, a Lord Mayor of London who helped to found the Bank of England, a world famous cycling champion, and the engineer of the Settle-Carlisle railway line. Colourful local characters include England's "super sandwich-board man" and one of the Midland's most celebrated poachers. On a more humble note are the interesting tombstones of mole catchers, macebearers, wrestlers, and rag and bone men. There are also gravestones with detailed medical histories, others which record accidents, and those which openly disagree with judicial decisions.

Individual entries are arranged chronologically under broad subject headings, with a certain amount of arbitration for characters who fit equally well into more than one section. In general, the scope of the book has been restricted to people whose tombs lie within the county of Leicestershire. Site locations are given in the text beneath each person's name. Exceptionally, where the term "commemorated" is used in a heading, it signifies the site of a memorial only, with the place of burial being elsewhere. Understandably, not everyone of interest could be included in the space available, whilst some unintentional omissions are inevitable.

As an aid to those doing their own research amongst Leicestershire's tombs, there is a practical Guide to Sources. This contains information not readily available in print elsewhere, and includes a guide to local authority cemetery records as well as an index to the recent Women's Institute graveyard surveys of the county.

Illustrations of tombstones and monuments accompany many of the entries. Amongst these are examples of the extremely attractive Swithland slate and Ketton headstones for which the county is famous, and anyone wishing to find out more about this fascinating industry will find suggestions for further reading at the end of the book.

Leicestershire churches, graveyards and monuments are well worth exploring, and it is the author's hope that this book will serve as a useful guide and itinerary for all those with an interest in this aspect of the past.

1. Unusual tombs and monuments

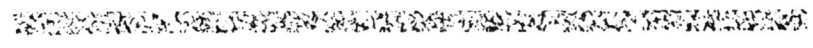

Francis Manners, 6th Earl of Rutland (1578-1632)
Bottesford, St. Mary

witchcraft and sorcery at Belvoir Castle

Tales of gloves dipped in hot water and rubbed against a cat called Rutterkin, of feathers boiled up in blood, of bewitched lovers and familiar spirits, all lie behind the unusual wording on Francis 6th Earl of Rutland's epitaph at Bottesford Church. Believed to be the only inscription of its kind in England, it claims that both the Earl's sons:

"DYED IN THEIR INFANCY BY WICKED PRACTISE & SORCERYE"

The case concerns the famous Belvoir Witches.

Shortly before the death of the Earl's first son in 1613, there had been trouble at Belvoir Castle over the dismissal of a local servant girl for dishonesty. Joan Flower, the girl's mother, was incensed by the accusation, and after complaining at the castle, went off cursing and shouting threats of revenge against the Earl and Countess.

Joan and her daughters were already regarded with suspicion by the other villagers, and after this episode increasingly became the subject of gossip concerning strange "goings on", lewd behaviour and witchcraft. It was not difficult in seventeenth century England to acquire a reputation as a witch: a few wrinkles, a squint, a peculiar voice and especially a fondness for cats, were all supposedly tell-tale signs. Once suspected, it was very difficult to lose the label, and any unpleasant events in the community tended to be blamed on the "witch".

Meanwhile the Manners family appeared to be increasingly stricken by sickness. As well as the strange illness and death of their first son Henry, the Earl and Countess were themselves afflicted. Their only daughter narrowly escaped death and their second son Francis was also taken very ill.

Suspicions began to grow that these events were due to something other than natural causes. Witchcraft was high on the list and in 1618 the chief local suspect Joan Flower, along with her daughters and several other local women, were rounded up and taken off to Lincoln gaol on charges of witchcraft and murder.

Joan's odd appearance, her reputation, fiery eyes and foul language can have done little to inspire confidence in her innocence. On the journey to Lincoln she is said to have asked for bread and butter, claiming that if she was guilty, God would choke her with it. She took a bite and

The "Witchcraft" tomb, Bottesford St. Mary

fell down dead instantly. Having known the fate that lay in store for her this was probably a case of self-administered poisoning. Whatever the explanation, the events dramatically sealed the fate of the others accused. Confessions of witchcraft were extracted and the verdict of guilty reached with its inevitable consequences.

Henry Lord Roos, the eldest of the two sons was buried at Bottesford, whilst his brother Francis was buried at Westminster Abbey. Their father's massive monument, upon which their unusual epitaph appears together with small effigies of both boys, is one of the outstanding series of monuments to the Earls of Rutland which stand inside St. Mary's at Bottesford. Reaching up to the ceiling, its height made the raising of the chancel roof necessary, and even then part of a rafter had to be cut out to accommodate the family peacock crest. The main part of Sir Francis' epitaph in the recess below this is a lengthy account of his travels abroad to the courts of foreign princes, emperors and counts. It also mentions his service to James I and Prince Charles (later Charles I), as well as his daughter's marriage to the Leicestershire-born royal favourite, George Villiers the Duke of Buckingham.

Other Leicestershire tombs with witchcraft associations include that of Ann Smith at Edmondthorpe and Richard Smith (q.v.) at Hinckley.

James Andrewe (1604-1638)
Leicester, St. Martin

anagrams in stone

The practice of making anagrams out of personal names to provide suitable inscriptions, appears to have enjoyed a certain amount of popularity during the seventeenth century. Some names lent themselves easily to anagrams. Others however produced rather more contrived results.

One of the most charming examples is a small relief memorial on the south wall of St. Dunstan's chapel at Leicester Cathedral. It commemorates James Andrewe and depicts him in his study with open books before him. Below are the lines:

> *"JAMES ANDREWE*
> *ANAGRAM*
> *REEDE I WAS MAN."*

A more lengthy inscription in Latin follows, part of which was originally engraved on a flat stone on the floor.

A less perfect anagram has been recorded at Castle Donnington:

> *"FERDINANDO HASTINGES*
> *OF GOD HE STANDS IN FEAR*
> *IS OF HIS NAME*
> *THE ANAGRAM*
> *SO OF HIS PIOUS MIND*
> *THE HAPPY CHARACTER,"*

The second line is almost, but not quite an anagram of the first. Ferdinando (d.1647) was the third son of the fifth Earl of Huntingdon.

In the southern part of the county at Church Langton the word ANAG is written in large letters on both sides of the monument to Thomas Stavelie (d.1631) which hangs high up on the north wall of the chancel of St. Peter's church. His name has been contrived to make "THESE MOST AVAILE". The Stavelies were lords of the manors of East and West Langton.

Anagram memorial to James Andrewe, Leicester St. Martin

Elias Travers (d.1641)
Thurcaston, All Saints

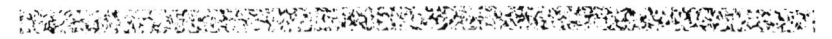

Leicestershire's oldest Swithland gravestone?

The earliest surviving post-Reformation churchyard memorials in Leicestershire belong to the seventeenth century. They are characteristically small thick rectangular upright stones, with short inscriptions giving only the briefest of details about the person commemorated. Decoration and ornamentation are rare.

The oldest known Swithland slate gravestone in the county is to be found at All Saints' Thurcaston. It commemorates Elias Travers, rector of Thurcaston from 1628 to 1641, and used to mark the site of his grave in the churchyard, but is now attached to a wall inside the church near the font. The stone is an irregular rectangle measuring approximately four feet high by one and a half feet wide, and has the words ". . AVERS DD OCTOBR 9TH 1641" still legible in large plain letters.

Theophilus Cave (1584-1656)
Barrow-upon-Soar, Holy Trinity

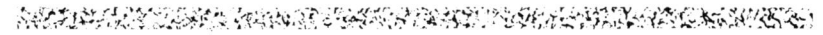

"If Cave be Grave and Grave be Cave"

An often cited example of seventeenth century grave humour is the verse on the Cave tablet at Holy Trinity, Barrow-upon-Soar:

> "HERE IN THIS GRAVE THERE LYES A CAVE.
> WE CALL A CAVE A GRAVE.
> IF CAVE BE GRAVE AND GRAVE BE CAVE.
> THEN READER JUDGE I CRAVE
> WHETHER DOTH CAVE HERE LYE IN GRAVE
> OR GRAVE HERE LYE IN CAVE?
> IF GRAVE IN CAVE HERE BURIED LYE
> THEN GRAVE WHERE IS THY VICTORIE?
> GOE READER AND REPORT HERE LYES A CAVE
> WHO CONQUERS DEATH AND BURIES HIS OWN GRAVE."

Almshouse at Barrow-upon-Soar, founded in memory of Theophilus Cave

This seemingly irreverent and now very indistinct inscription can be found in the chancel on the small section of Theophilus Cave's monument between the upper and lower tablets.

Theophilus himself is reputed to have been an ardent and devout churchman, and it was to his memory that the almshouse opposite the lychgate was founded in 1694 through the wishes of his nephew Humphrey Babington. Originally a one storey thatched building, it has subsequently been altered and extended. The poor men whom the charity supported were known as the Bedesmen of Theophilus Cave and were provided with shelter, clothing, fuel and money to buy food. Strict rules governed their conduct. They were required to be inside by seven o'clock for supper every night, and ready for prayers by eight. The doors were closed at nine. Good behaviour was expected, with riotous or disorderly conduct leading to banishment. The Bedesmen were to be seen in church on Sunday clad in the blue and cream gowns of the charity up until the 1930's. They had their own door to enter by and their own seats in the chancel. Today the charity continues although its beneficiaries are no longer referred to as Bedesmen and both men and women are eligible. Further information about its foundation appears on two large boards inside the church.

Baptist Noel, 3rd Viscount Campden (d.1683)
Exton, St. Peter and St. Paul

from Chipping Campden to Exton

The rural church of St. Peter and St. Paul at Exton, four miles north-east of Oakham, houses some of the finest monuments in the country. Visually, the most impressive is that to Baptist Noel, 3rd Viscount Campden. Not only is it one of the best works of the famous sculptor Grinling Gibbons, but also an extraordinary monument of enormous size. The story starts not at Exton, but down in Gloucestershire.

Visitors to the picturesque Cotswold town of Chipping Campden may have been intrigued by glimpses of twirling ornate pinnacled chimney stacks, domed gatehouses, pavilions, and ruined walls, which clearly mark the site of a house of substance. These are the remains of Campden House, formerly a beautiful Italianate-style building. It was built for Sir Baptist Hicks, 1st Lord Campden, a wealthy London merchant and money-lender, who came to Chipping Campden at the beginning of the seventeenth century. When he died in 1629, the property passed through marriage to Sir Edward Noel, afterwards 2nd Viscount Campden, whose family owned estates in Leicestershire and Rutland.

The Noel connections with Campden House were however short-lived. The English Civil War intervened and the house was garrisoned. Later the building was either accidentally or deliberately destroyed by fire. Sir Edward who was a royalist supporter died during the war. His monument erected at Campden after the Restoration is one of the best known in the country. The title of Viscount Campden then passed to Sir Edward's son Baptist Noel, who with Campden Hall in ruins, returned to the East Midlands. The Noel family retained some of their links with Chipping Campden. Many of their local benefactions survive, and the old arched market hall in the High Street remained a family possession until 1942, when it passed into the hands of the National Trust, narrowly escaping being dismantled and shipped off to America.

Baptist Noel's monument at Exton is a spectacular piece of sepulchral architecture. Standing some twenty-two feet high and fourteen feet wide, it reaches up to the ceiling of the church, almost filling one wall of the north transept. In the centre, on either side of a pedestalled urn, are the larger than life figures of the Viscount and his fourth wife. Very much a family memorial, it also depicts his three previous wives, and all nineteen of his children! It cost £1,000 and was erected in 1686, three years after his death. By this time, it was evidently felt to be safe to put up royalist inscriptions and tell of family misfortunes during the Civil War:

"HERE RESTETH BAPTIST NOEL, LORD VISCOUNT CAMPDEN, BARON OF RIDLINGTON AND ILMINGTON, LORD LIEUTENTANT OF THE COUNTY OF RUTLAND. HIS EMINENT LOYALTY TO HIS TWO SOVEREIGNS, KING CHARLES I AND II; HIS CONJUGAL AFFECTION TO FOUR WIVES; HIS PATERNAL INDULGENCE TO NINETEEN CHILDREN; HIS HOSPITALITY AND LIBERALITY TO ALL THAT DESIRED OR DESERVED IT (NOTWITHSTANDING INESTIMABLE LOSSES IN HIS ESTATE, FREQUENT IMPRISONMENTS OF HIS PERSON, SPOIL AND HAVOCK OF SEVERAL OF HIS HOUSES, BESIDES THE BURNING OF THAT NOBLE PILE OF CAMPDEN), HAVE JUSTLY RENDRED HIM THE ADMIRATION OF HIS CONTEMPORARIES AND THE IMITATION OF POSTERITY."

Exton Hall where the family used to live has long since been destroyed by fire, but traces of its ruins are still clearly visible between Exton Church and the present hall.

Baptist Noel's 22 feet high monument, Exton St. Peter and St. Paul

Robert Swann (d.1749)
Belton-in-Rutland, St. Peter

denied a burial place

Whilst many of the nonconformist sects used Anglican churchyards, the Quakers deliberately shunned them, establishing and using their own burial grounds from an early date. In general, the Quakers also opposed the custom of erecting monuments and gravestones, considering this to be a show of vanity and personal pride.

Robert Swann however was a member of the Society who was buried in Church of England ground, and also commemorated there. His unusual epitaph at Belton Church describing the circumstances which brought this about used to read:

> "NEAR THIS PLACE INTERRED THERE LIES,
> ONE WHOM THE QUAKERS DID DESPISE.
> HIS POVERTY EARNED HIM DISGRACE,
> THEY DENIED HIM A BURIAL PLACE:
> THOUGH BY HIS FRIEND, IT HATH BEEN SAID,
> TOWARDS A BURYING PLACE LARGE SUMS WERE PAID,
> POOR ROBERT MIGHT NOT THERE BE LAID.
> OH FRIENDS, HOW COULD YOU BE SO HARD,
> TO LET HIM LIE IN THIS CHURCHYARD;
> A PLACE YOU ALL DISLIKE, WE KNOW,
> HOW COULD YOU DISPLACE A BROTHER SO.
> IN MEMORY HERE THIS STONE DOTH STAND,
> OF ROBERT, THE SON OF JOHN AND SARAH SWANN.
> IN ONE THOUSAND SEVEN HUNDRED AND FORTY NINE
> HE DID HIS SOUL TO GOD RESIGN."

Unfortunately many of the stones in the churchyard have weathered badly and this inscription like many others there is almost illegible.

Sir Joseph Danvers (1686-1753)
Swithland, St. Leonard

one man and his dog

Sir Joseph Danvers' monument is one of the most unusual in Leicestershire. It is a large railed-off box tomb built into the churchyard wall of St. Leonard's at Swithland. According to tradition, Sir Joseph wished not to be buried inside the church because he could not bear to be separated from his favourite dog. Instead he had his tomb built partly inside the churchyard and partly outside, so that he could lie in consecrated ground and his dog could lie close by in unconsecrated ground. Inscribed on the tomb are the words "Bodys Guard 1745". Sir Joseph was a Member of Parliament for many years, a Deputy Lieutenant and a Justice of the Peace.

Sir Joseph Danvers' tomb built into Swithland churchyard wall

The monument is also well worth seeing for the finely carved pictorial slate reliefs which decorate two sides of the tomb. One is a scene showing ploughing and building activities, and has the inscription:

"BE CHEARFULL OH MAN AND LABOUR TO LIVE
THE MERCIFULL GOD A BLESSING WILL GIVE."

The other shows a ship at sea, with a church and hills in the background, and has the lines:

"WHEN YOUNG I SAYL'D TO INDIA EAST AND WEST,
BUT AGED IN THIS PORT MUST LYE AT REST."

Finely carved Swithland slate detail from Sir Joseph Danvers' tomb

Edwards Family (18th and 19th centuries)
Welham, St. Andrew

one of England's richest heiresses

Currently housed in the north transept of St. Andrew's at Welham, is a structure once described as one of the finest outdoor monuments in Europe. Costing £1,500, it was commissioned by the eccentric Mary Edwards, in memory of her father Francis Edwards, and originally stood in the churchyard outside the east window. The monument weathered badly and following cleaning and restoration at Stamford, was resited early in the nineteenth century in the newly constructed mausoleum on the north side of the church.

Francis Edwards was responsible for rebuilding much of Welham village in the eighteenth century. He also had plans to run the Leicester to London turnpike road right through the village, accommodating travellers at a splendid new inn. Support for his scheme proved difficult to find, and the intended inn was converted into a mansion instead. Even this was short-lived, and within forty years had fallen into a ruinous state. Today only the walls and gate piers remain. Not far away, in a field opposite the present-day inn, a series of depressions in the land can be seen. These mark the site of an ornamental canal, another project probably designed with his dutch wife in mind.

Mary inherited an enormous fortune from her father. It made her one of the richest heiresses in England and proved a great attraction for many fortune hunters. One such was the spendthrift Lord Ann Hamilton, a handsome guardsman and the younger son of James the 4th Duke of Hamilton who had been killed in a duel in Hyde park in 1713. Lord Ann completely turned Mary's head and the two were hastily married in London in 1731. In 1732 Mary bore him a son Gerard Ann. Meanwhile Lord Ann's increasingly heavy demands on her purse were beginning to cause problems. Unprotected in law and anxious to safeguard her fortune for her son, Mary took a remarkable course. She effaced all trace of their marriage from the Fleet registers and had her son's baptism recorded at St. Mary Abbot's Kensington as the child of a single woman. The plan worked. Mary recovered her property and was separated from Lord Ann in 1734.

Mary was one of William Hogarth's earliest patrons. She commissioned various works from him including the unflattering portrait of her son, currently on display at Upton House in Warwickshire. She also commissioned his more famous work "Taste a la mode", intending it as a satirical attack on London's fashionable society who made fun of her country ways and eccentric manner. Hogarth's work was not to everyone's taste, and his supporters, including Mary, were considered by many to be distinctly odd.

In 1743 Mary died aged thirty-eight and was buried alongside her father at Welham. Through her will she left the bulk of her estate to her son and various legacies to her servants. Provision was also made for the upkeep of the family monument at Welham, with orders that her own funeral be conducted "without plumes or escutcheons . . . and in all respects as private as is consistent with decency".

Mary's son married Lady Jane Noel, daughter of the 9th Earl of Gainsborough. Both names of the couple are to be found on the Welham monument. Lady Jane's funeral contrasted strongly with that of her mother-in-law where according to contemporary reports, the body lay in state at Ketton for seven days, during which time some 3,000 people came to pay their last respects. Afterwards the procession of:

". . . mutes, horsemen, and pages, the state lid of black ostrich feathers, the hearse with six horses, richly dressed with feathers, velvets, escutcheons, streamers, pendants, schraffoons, with all the pomp and paraphernalia in vogue, followed by three hundred mounted tenants with gloves, scarves and hatbands . . ." made its way along the sixteen mile route from Ketton to Welham. At Welham, while the service was proceeding, the coffin complete with its plumes was slowly lowered into the vault.

An early illustration of the Edwards Family monument which once dominated Welham churchyard (from Nichols' "Leicestershire")

Fortrey Family (18th century)
King's Norton, St. John the Baptist

Billesdon's loss – King's Norton's gain

A contemporary monument of a similar but less elaborate design to the Edwards' memorial at Welham, can be found about eight miles away in the churchyard of St. John the Baptist, King's Norton. Hidden from the road, but clearly visible from inside the church as a towering shadowy outline, it stands at the rear of the building immediately outside the east window. Over fifteen feet high, it is one of the tallest outdoor monuments in the county. Four balls above a large stepped base support a tall obelisk, on top of which is an urn. The badly weathered inscription on the base indicates that it commemorates the parents of William Fortrey.

William Fortrey, at whose expense it was erected, was the local squire. Like many eighteenth century gentlemen, he had a passion for building projects, and rebuilt the attractive St. Peter's church at Gaulby. Another plan was to rebuild Billesdon Church, but "about the second walk he took for the purpose of fixing on an eligible spot, he happened to trespass upon a surly man's grounds, who came upon him unawares, and with unbecoming language threatened to put him into the pinfold". So disconcerted was Fortrey that he turned his attention elsewhere and as a result rebuilt the magnificent church of St. John's at King's Norton.

Afterwards he planned to build a new hall at King's Norton, but died when the scheme was barely off the drawing board. His funeral took place in the village on 19th December 1783. Although Fortrey's own name was never added to his parents' monument as he originally intended, St. John's Church itself serves as his finest memorial.

The decorative wrought iron gates from the old hall now grace the entrance to the churchyard. Close by on the wall is a Silver Jubilee plaque erected by Harborough District Council in 1977, which as well as commemorating the rebuilding of the church, also records William Fortrey's enthusiasm for campanology.

Other obelisk-shaped memorials in the same part of the county can be seen at Hallaton and Carlton Curlieu. Both commemorate local eighteenth century rectors. That at Hallaton is to the Reverend George Fenwicke (d.1760) and is actually built onto an outside wall of the church. The similar, but smaller version at Carlton Curlieu commemorating the Reverend William Fenwicke (d.1733) is a free standing structure. The Fenwickes came from Northumberland, as do the Fenwicks connected with the well-known Leicester store of the same name.

James Wigley (c.1700-1765)
Scraptoft, All Saints

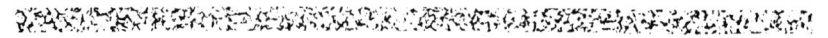

an eighteenth century job creation scheme

One of the more unusually illustrated wall memorials in the county is to be found not far from Leicester at All Saints' Scraptoft. It shows James Wigley, five times Member of Parliament for Leicester and owner of Scraptoft Hall, supervising workers planting trees on his estate. In reality the project not only beautified the grounds of Scraptoft Hall, but also helped create jobs for the unemployed. Afterwards, Wigley and his successors opened up the grounds to the public, providing "a treat to

Leicester people of all descriptions".

Today the hall and grounds are part of the Leicester Polytechnic. Some of Wigley's plantations can still be seen, as can other landscape features, including a shell-lined grotto, and a tall artificial mound on which once stood a belvedere.

His epitaph at Scraptoft concludes:

"BUT LET NOT INGRATITUDE BURY IN OBLIVION HIS BOUNTY TO HIS TENANTS, AND NOBLE SPIRIT IN ENCOURAGING THE HONEST INDUSTRY OF THE POOR;
TO BE SILENT HERE WOULD BE A WRONG TO HIS MEMORY AND THE PUBLICK: TO SAY MORE, IN THIS PLACE, IS UNNECESSARY."

The entrance to James Wigley's grotto at Scraptoft

Detail from James Wigley's monument, Scraptoft All Saints

William Squire (d.1781)
Burton Lazars, St. James

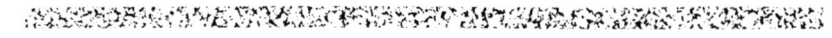

a slight miscalculation

A few miles from the outskirts of Melton is one of the largest and most ambitious churchyard monuments in the county. Standing some twenty feet high and clearly visible from the Melton to Oakham road, it dominates the north-west corner of Burton Lazars churchyard. Originally gilded and painted to imitate marble, it would once have looked even more impressive.

It commemorates William Squire, an eighteenth century weaver, who by the time of his death on 1st October 1781, had amassed a small fortune of around £600. His intentions had been for part of this sum to be spent on a memorial to himself and his parents, part to provide the means for its upkeep, and the remainder to be used to help educate poor children. Unfortunately he miscalculated. The monument cost far more than he had allowed for, and by the time it was complete there was little left over for the charity.

Throsby and Nichols, the county's two leading historians, both commented on the monument whilst in its original, glistening condition. Noting its conspicuous appearance, Nichols wrote:

> "The tomb and sarcophagus stand on an oval base, which support, by four balls, a pyramid; in the centre of which, pierced through, is an ornamented urn; and on the top stand on a ball two eagles, with serpents in their mouths entwined round an urn and flame. On the East end, the figures of the heavenly bodies on a globe, surrounded by a snake biting his tail, the emblem of Eternity. Underneath, are compartments containing a skull, the cross, I.H.S. the glory, &c. On the west end, the globe the same; and the compartments, a skull and bones. On the sarcophagus, figures of Time, Faith, Hope, &c. and on the pyramid, the censer, instruments of the Passion, &c."

Throsby was far less polite finding it altogether too showy and gaudy a structure:

> "... a gingerbread tomb... the baseless fabric of a vision... Upon this partly-coloured pile are urns, arms, and leg-bones tied together with a cord, hanging pendant from a jaw-bone, I had almost said, of an ass. It abounds with imitations of skulls, angels, crosses and glories."

A more recent opinion considers that for those who want to see a monument which has everything, "this, surely is it!".

William Squire's eccentric monument in Burton Lazars churchyard

ABCD Tombstone
Newtown Linford, All Saints

a Newtown Linford mystery

A curiosity at Newtown Linford Church is a small stone about fifteen inches by three feet known as the "ABCD tombstone". It bears no name, merely the letters of the alphabet, perfectly inscribed in both small and capital letters, along with two incomplete sets of Arabic numerals. The stone used to stand in the churchyard but it has recently been moved inside and attached to the wall behind the font. One local story says that it was put in accordance with the will of an eccentric inhabitant who wanted the alphabet and numbers on his tomb, so that "persons who come to look at it might make anything they liked from it". Another story says it was an apprentice mason's pattern slab sold to a poor illiterate man for a memorial stone.

The "ABCD" tombstone, All Saints Newtown Linford

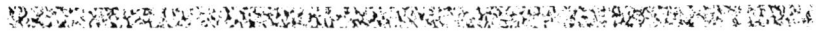

Sarah Johnson (d. 1819)
Loughborough, Woodgate Baptist Church
(Memorial now in the Old Rectory Museum, Loughborough).

Esther Houghton (d.1797)
Saxelbye, St. Peter

tapped for 310 gallons

Amongst the more unusually inscribed gravestones, are those which provide a record of the deceased's medical treatment. One of the diseases which merited such attention was ascites (dropsy), a condition which caused liquid to build up in the body and required the excess to be "tapped" or drained away.

Esther Houghton and Sarah Johnson were two young sufferers of the disease, both of whose gravestones record the phenomenal amounts of liquid which had to be removed. Sarah's stone used to stand in the yard of Loughborough's Woodgate Baptist Church and is now preserved in the Rectory Museum. It tabulates her operations, recording the amounts of fluid taken away by Dr Brown and Dr Vickers on each of twenty-eight separate occasions. Details of the costs incurred can be read on the notice above the stone. By the time Sarah finally succumbed at the age of twenty-eight she had been tapped for 310 gallons, 1 quart, 1 pint over a period of six years, on average almost a gallon a week. It is not known who carved the stone since its broken off base is still in the ground, nor is it known who paid for it, Sarah's own family having been in receipt of financial assistance from the parish.

A slightly earlier stone at Saxelbye carved by Winfield recalls how Esther Houghton was "tap'd 21 times from August the 21st 1789, to April the 28th 1797. The Quantity of Water taken from her was 222 Gallons, weighing 19 c. 2 qrs. 9 lbs."

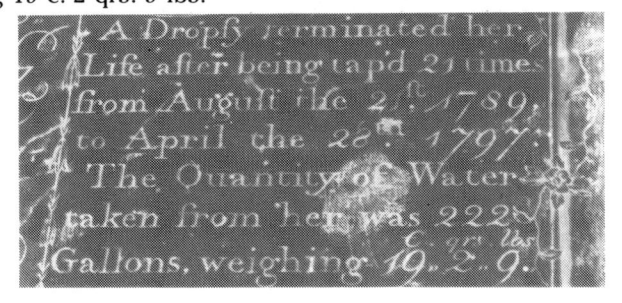

Details of Esther Houghton's treatment at Saxelbye St. Peter

Sarah Johnson's unusual medical record at Loughborough

Rose Boswell (d.1794)
South Luffenham, St. Mary

Absalom Smith (d.1826)
Twyford, St. Andrew

Aaron Boswell (d.1866)
Long Whatton, All Saints

a towering palisade over six feet high

Until the turn of this century, many gypsy families followed the practice of burying their dead in unconsecrated ground, favouring heathland, edges of woods and wayside ditches. Other families however, preferred burial in Christian ground, often choosing locations situated close to hedgerows. Wooden posts driven into the ground and specially planted thorn bushes, as well as more conventional monuments were used to mark such sites.

When a gypsy died, the female relatives would keep vigil by the body until the funeral, custom usually allowing viewing by friends and relatives. During this period it was also usual for the adult relatives to fast, the cooking of food and even the eating of cooked food, especially red meat, being regarded as taboo. The fast would end when the mourners returned from the graveside, after the funeral. Since touching the dead was similarly taboo, the laying out of the body was usually carried out by gorgios (non-gypsies). Normally the deceased was buried fully dressed, and in the Midlands the wearing of shoes was not uncommon. Coffins were frequently large enough to allow room for many of the deceased's possessions, such as clothes, jewellery, walking stick, tankard and other personal items.

After the burial came the sacrifice, the best known and most publicised part of gypsy funeral customs, in which most of the remaining property of the deceased was spectacularly destroyed. Waggons, carts, furniture, bedding and clothing were burnt in a blazing pyre; crockery, pots, dishes and mirrors were smashed to pieces and other sacrifices made. Following the funeral of Aaron Boswell at Long Whatton in Leicestershire in 1866 his clothes, tent, cart, harness and other goods were burned. His pots and pans were broken up and then buried in the ground. Since the mourners were not themselves allowed to sell his horses or any remaining possessions, a man from outside the family was given this task.

One Christmas almost three-quarters of a century earlier, members of a branch of the same tribe were camped on a heath just outside South Luffenham. The party's stay there was lengthened by the sickness of their leader's consumptive daughter who had become too ill to move on. The cruel winter weather worsened her condition, and when it became clear that she had not much longer to live, large numbers of people started gathering at the camp to witness her last moments. She died 9th February 1794, and it was the wish of her people that she be buried at South Luffenham Parish Church. Initially the churchwardens objected to the burial of a non-Christian in Christian ground, but were eventually persuaded to agree. A note in the parish register draws attention to the fact that "The above young woman was one of the people commonly called 'Gipsies', (she) was buried in the church and had a funeral sermon preached". A few weeks later a marble stone slab arrived from London and was placed over her remains. This stone can be found in the south aisle near to the organ. Its inscription, now barely legible, reads:

*"IN MEMORY OF
ROSE BOSWELL
DAUGHTER OF EDWARD AND SARAH BOSWELL
WHO DIED FEBRUARY 19TH 1794
AGE 17 YEARS.
WHAT GRIEF CAN VENT THIS LOSS OR PRAISES TELL,
HOW MEEK, HOW GOOD, HOW BEAUTIFUL SHE FELL."*

Gypsy deaths are also recorded locally in the parish records of Markfield and Barrow-upon-Soar, but the most famous gypsy buried in Leicestershire is Absalom Smith, a popular gypsy 'King' of the last century. A tall man of dark complexion and black hair with long curls on each side of his face, he generally wore a long silver-buttoned blue coat, breeches, leggings and silver-buckled shoes. Well-known especially for his abilities on the fiddle, he was a great favourite at local fairs and village wakes, where he would play for dances well into the early hours of the morning.

It was during one such session at the tap room of the Saddle Inn at Twyford, that he was taken ill, or according to another story was badly wounded in a fight. Dr Noble, the eminent Leicester physician was called out, but despite his care Absalom died on 10th February 1826 at the age of sixty.

According to tradition, Absalom was buried in his 'royal' clothes. He also wore a pair of silver-buckled shoes, each buckle reputedly weighing half a pound. Straw and timber were put on the coffin which had been made by local carpenter John Baines. Gypsies from a dozen camps attended the funeral, at which in addition to the usual church service, "all the peculiar ceremonies of the tribe were performed". Afterwards, his tent, bedding, panniers and fiddle were all burnt. He left behind a widow, thirteen children, one hundred and four grandchildren, and a fortune that amounted to a gallon of sovereigns.

His burial place lies near to St. Andrew's churchyard wall, just inside the entrance gate, in an area now clear of gravestones. Originally the site was marked by a towering palisade over six feet high, but this has long since been removed. The grave was reported to have been accidentally disturbed in 1890, but no trace of any grave goods were found.

Colonel Edward Cheney (1778-1848)
Gaddesby, St. Luke

action from the Battle of Waterloo

The most noticeable monument inside St. Luke's at Gaddesby is an unusual and almost lifesize statue of a horse and rider, which occupies a prominent position in the chancel. Excluding cathedrals, only three similar statues are known to exist in English churches. It was not however originally intended as a church monument, since after having been brought by cart from Leicester to Gaddesby it was kept for a number of years in a conservatory at Gaddesby Hall. Then in the early part of this century, about 1917, horse and rider were put on rollers and dragged by ropes through the grounds of the hall to the church.

Carved by Joseph Gott in white Italian marble, the monument commemorates Colonel Edward Cheney. It shows him on his most famous day of action at the Battle of Waterloo, when he had four horses killed under him and a fifth wounded, all within the space of twenty-four hours. Other scenes from the battle are depicted on the base below the statue.

The Colonel married a Leicestershire lady, and after a distinguished military career, retired to Gaddesby. There he became a prominent member of Melton's hunting society. The local press lamented his death in 1848, noting that he had been a fine specimen of the "old English officer", and also a man who although of a historical family, had none of the pride of descent about him, being a staunch, consistent, and long-known friend of the rights of the people.

Colonel Cheney in action, Gaddesby St. Luke

Richard Twining (1807-1906)
Bitteswell, St. Mary

an unusual Midlands monument

Graveboards are an unusual type of wooden memorial which are most commonly found in the churchyards of the Home Counties and the South-East. They are rare in the Midlands, and it comes as something of a surprise when walking round the back of Bitteswell churchyard, to find a well preserved example near the corner of the building. It consists of a horizontal board supported a short way above ground level by a post or 'bedhead' at either end. Dating from earlier this century, it commemorates Richard Twining, a member of the "Twinings Tea" family who came to live at Bitteswell during his retirement. There is a further memorial to him at the cemetery on the Ullesthorpe Road which commemorates his gift of the land for the cemetery. He also gave the lychgate to St. Mary's, presenting it in memory of the Reverend James Powell, Bitteswell's longest serving vicar, after whom Powell Row in the village is named (q.v. Mary Powell).

Wooden graveboard in Bitteswell churchyard

Joseph Hayes (d.1886)
Helen Hayes (d.1914)
Wymondham, St. Peter

photographs in Wymondham churchyard

The custom of displaying photographs on monuments is far more common on the Continent than in England. Where examples are found here it is noticeable that the majority are recent and that many are memorials to people from abroad who have settled in this country.

In the north-eastern part of Leicestershire however, is an earlier and more unusual example of this practice, which can be seen amongst the headstones now lined up against the eastern wall of Wymondham churchyard. Unlike current techniques which usually incorporate a weather-resistant photograph into an oval convex form, the stone at Wymondham has two small niches hollowed out of it. Inside, protected from the elements by glass, are photographs commemorating Joseph and Helen Hayes.

Gravestone incorporating photographs, Wymondham St. Peter

Christopher Gardner (1916-1924)
Newton Harcourt, St. Luke

a unique miniature church

Quite close to the gate leading into St. Luke's churchyard, is a very unusual and possibly unique memorial. Standing only a few feet high, it is a three-dimensional miniature church, which has been carved complete with a Norman doorway, battlements, a spire and even traceried windows. Erected early this century, it commemorates a young boy called Christopher Gardner.

A miniature church in Newton Harcourt churchyard

Morpeth Webb (1861-1930)
Burton Lazars, St. James

portrait of a painter of miniatures

Artist Morpeth Webb's gravestone lies between the Zborowski family enclosure and William Squire's notable monument (q.v.) in the northwest part of St. James' churchyard, Burton Lazars. It is unconventional for an outside monument in that it bears a small round copper medallion engraved with a portrait of the deceased. The initials R.M.S. indicate that Webb specialised in painting miniatures.

Morpeth Webb's portrait in Burton Lazars churchyard

35

2. Scientists, engineers and doctors

Vincent Wing (1619-1668)
North Luffenham, St. John the Baptist

astrological forecasts which sold 50,000 copies a year

North Luffenham's most celebrated inhabitant was Vincent Wing, a talented mathematician and astronomer. Although lacking a university education, he was not only able to hold his own with the best scholars of the day, but he also had a much better understanding of the Copernican System than many of his contemporaries. His highly regarded astronomical almanacs made him a national name, and were considered by the future Astronomer Royal John Flamsteed to be the most accurate tables available.

Like many seventeenth century astronomers, Wing also dabbled in astrology making various prognostications to satisfy the demands of a credulous and superstitious age. He made his forecasts available in a number of popular publications, one of which sold a phenomenal 50,000 copies annually. It is also said that he correctly forecast his own death, having made out his will just a fortnight before. His remains were interred at North Luffenham. Afterwards, his work was carried on by his descendants, one of whom was Tycho Wing, a great friend of the noted antiquarian William Stukeley.

Reverend Thomas Daffy (d.1680)
Redmile, St. Peter

the inventor of "Daffy's Elixir"

In 1618 the first "London Pharmacopoeia" appeared. It contained nearly 2,000 remedies for treating diseases, with recipes including such ingredients as the dried lungs of foxes, animal dung, crab's eyes, animal hooves and moss scraped from the skull of a convicted criminal. Such were the treatments available for the seventeenth century doctor to practise on a population that firmly believed in the influence of astrology, palmistry and witchcraft on life.

Thomas Daffy was a Leicestershire clergyman of this period who invented one of the most celebrated and popular cure-all medicines of the seventeenth and eighteenth centuries. Known as "Daffy's Elixir", the potion was probably first mixed in the Vale of Belvoir where Daffy was rector of Harby and later Redmile. It was claimed, and no doubt believed by many, to be a remedy for all manner of ills, from pains, colic, gout and scurvy, to cleansing the blood, preventing miscarriages and destroying worms. Whilst such claims would now be regarded with scepticism, the medicine's properties to provide "cheerful" relief to sufferers long maintained its popularity amongst customers throughout the country. Newspaper advertisements show that versions of the original were still going strong over a hundred years after Daffy's death. Whatever ingredients Daffy used can only be imagined as the recipe was a closely guarded family secret.

Daffy died in 1680 and was buried at Redmile Church, where today there is little to recall his once national fame.

Advertisement from the "Leicester Journal" 1797 for the popular cure-all medicine invented by a Leicestershire clergyman

Reverend Andrew Glen (c.1666-1732)
Hathern, St. Peter and St. Paul

a collection of over a thousand dried plants

Serious research into Leicestershire botany started in the eighteenth century with Loughborough-born Richard Pulteney being the most famous of the early pioneers. Other early botanists of note with local connections include the Reverend Andrew Glen of Hathern. Shortly after graduating from Cambridge, Glen achieved the considerable feat of collecting a substantial herbarium of around 1,000 dried plants, gathered from all over Britain and the Continent. Later, several hundred more specimens were added following a visit to Italy. He was also a friend of the distinguished botanist John Ray, sending him specimens from Leicestershire to help with his work. Glen is buried at St. Peter's Church, Hathern where he was vicar from 1694 to his death in 1732.

James Sherard (1666-1737)
Evington, St. Denys

one of the finest botanical gardens in England

In the early eighteenth century, Eltham in Kent possessed a noted botanic garden considered by many to be one of the finest in England. The garden was largely the work of distinguished Leicestershire botanist James Sherard.

Born at Bushby, Sherard trained as a pharmacist in London under Charles Watts, who was also the curator of Chelsea Botanical Gardens. Afterwards he ran his own apothecary's business in London's Mark Lane, periodically exhibiting rare plants there. He also organised botanical excursions, including this one in 1714 with a Mr Petiver:

> "from London to Riverhead, Sevenoaks and Tunbridge Wells; and thence, in a chaise with two horses, 24 miles (through such horrid and deep roads by Tilehurst and Woodhurst as no coach or chaise had ever passed) after many hard tugs to Brede; afterwards to Hastings; Winchelsea (where they were entertained at the mayor's house, and the place not affording any wine, regaled with excellent punch made by the mayoress, every bowl of which was better than the former one); Rye, Lydd, New Romney, Sandgate Castle; Folkestone (a base rugged town, inhabited only by fishermen); Dover, Waldeshare, Knowlton, Deal, Sandwich, Isle of Thanet, Canterbury, Feversham, the marshes near Shepey, Rochester and Northfleet."
>
> (John Nichols)

Business prospered making him a sizeable fortune and in 1720 he retired to live in Eltham. There he established his outstanding collection of plants which became noted for its rare species gathered from all over the world. Retaining his links with Leicestershire, he purchased land in the county including the Manor of Evington (which according to Throsby had been gambled away by the Duke of Devonshire), and when he died he was buried there in the Parish Church of St. Denys. A marble wall memorial in the church's chancel praises his many talents. His brother William Sherard, also a botanist, endowed a professorial chair of botany at Oxford University.

Robert Pull (d.1755)
Market Bosworth, St. Peter

Pull's pills for the multitude

The eighteenth century was the golden age of patent medicines, wonder cures and quacks, and with no proper register controlling those who practised medicine, characters like Market Bosworth's highly regarded "Doctor" Pull flourished all over the country. According to Throsby, no man stood higher in the opinion of the "open-mouthed pill swallowing multitude". The brief inscription on Pull's gravestone remarks on his sudden departure at the age of sixty. Local legend suggests that he was buried alive!

The stone is now almost hidden, and lies in St. Peter's churchyard, east of the south porch, at the foot of the yew trees, a short distance beyond the more prominent flat granite slab to scholar and writer Arthur Benoni Evans.

William Whiston (1667-1752)
Lyndon, St. Martin

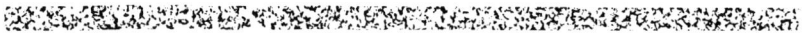

successor to Newton as Professor of Mathematics

Amongst the gravestones now lined up against the churchyard wall at Lyndon is one upon which the name William Whiston can still just be read. Whiston, a native of Norton-juxta-Twycross was a famous scholar of mathematics, astronomy and theology. He is best remembered as one of the first to popularise Sir Isaac Newton's theories, and for his translation of the Jewish historian Josephus.

The possessor of a brilliant, if sometimes unbalanced intellect, Whiston graduated from Cambridge in 1693 and after several clerical appointments was chosen to succeed Newton as Professor of Mathematics at Cambridge in 1703. Seven years later he was dismissed because of his controversial religious views and went to live in London, supporting himself largely by freelance lecturing, tutoring and writing. Gifts from friends and patrons, including £40 a year from the wife of George II, also helped out. There he became one of the first, if not the very first, to accompany lectures with experiments. He is also believed to have originated the expression "Northern Lights" for the phenomenon known as the Aurora Borealis. His prolific writings include over fifty major works. He was also involved in a multitude of projects, including a detailed survey of the coastline which he claimed to be the most complete of its time.

Although never received back into the academic community at Cambridge, Whiston remained intellectually active into his eighties. He died on 22nd August 1752 whilst visiting his daughter at Lyndon Hall and was buried close by at St. Martin's beside his wife.

Thomas Simpson (1710-1761)
Sutton Cheney, St. James

discoverer of Simpson's Rule

The prominent wall memorial situated just inside the entrance to St. James' Sutton Cheney with a Latin inscription by scholar and writer Arthur Benoni Evans, commemorates mathematician Thomas Simpson. According to an early edition of "Encyclopaedia Britannica" Simpson was a man who would long be considered the most illustrious on the lengthy roll of non-academic British mathematicians. He is best remembered for giving his name to Simpson's Rule, a method for calculating areas under curves which is still widely used today. However, astrology rather than mathematics first made his name.

Humbly born at Market Bosworth and a weaver by trade, he successfully learnt how to make a living casting horoscopes whilst lodging at Nuneaton. Popularly known as "The Oracle of Nuneaton, Bosworth and environs", his forecasts were in great demand. Couples would not marry, nor people do important business without consulting him first. However, reports that he had frightened a young girl into a fit by "raising the devil" (in reality a friend dressed up), cost him his reputation and he was forced to flee to Derby. Abandoning fortune-telling he next moved to London where he worked hard establishing himself as an extremely talented and serious amateur mathematician. In 1740 he was elected to the Royal Academy of Stockholm. Three years later he became Professor of Mathematics at the Royal Academy at Woolwich and in 1745 was appointed a fellow of the Royal Society. His work includes reports on the plans for London's Blackfriars Bridge as well as many mathematical papers.

Later in life, suffering from poor health and depression, he returned to Leicestershire, but died very shortly afterwards and was buried in Sutton Cheney churchyard. Leicestershire historian John Throsby visited the site some thirty years later and finding no memorial, ordered a small stone to be placed there and inscribed:

> "THE REMAINS OF THE BOSWORTH PRODIGY,
> THOMAS SIMPSON, F.R.S. REST IN THIS CHURCHYARD.
> AFTER RENDING ASSUNDER THE FETTERS OF INDIGENCE,
> HE AROSE TO AN ENVIED EMINENCE AS A MATHEMATICIAN;
> AND DIED A.D. 1761.
> J. THROSBY, ON AN EXCURSION IN LEICESTERSHIRE IN 1790,
> SEEING HIS NEGLECTED GRAVE,
> CAUSED THIS TABLET TO BE ERECTED TO HIS MEMORY."

There is no trace of this or any other stone to Simpson in the churchyard now, but the 1834 memorial inside the church is easily found.

Lewis Powel Williams (1732-1771)
Kibworth, St. Wilfrid

a curious medical claim at Kibworth

Hanging on an outside wall near the south porch of St. Wilfrid's Church Kibworth is an attractive but curiously worded memorial. It commemorates Lewis Powel Williams, an elusive surgeon who according to the inscription was the first person who

> "INTRODUCED INTO PRACTICE INOCULATION WITHOUT PREPARATION IN THIS KINGDOM."

This is believed to be a reference to the treatment of smallpox, although precisely what he did remains a mystery. The accuracy of the claim must be in some doubt as Lady Mary Wortley Montagu is usually recognised as being the first to introduce variolation into this country. Also, the Dorset farmer Benjamin Jesty and London physician Dr. Edward Jenner are normally considered to have discovered the use of cowpox as a smallpox vaccine.

Ironically, a century later, it was Leicester that became the centre of the anti-vaccination movement! (q.v. Amos Booth).

41

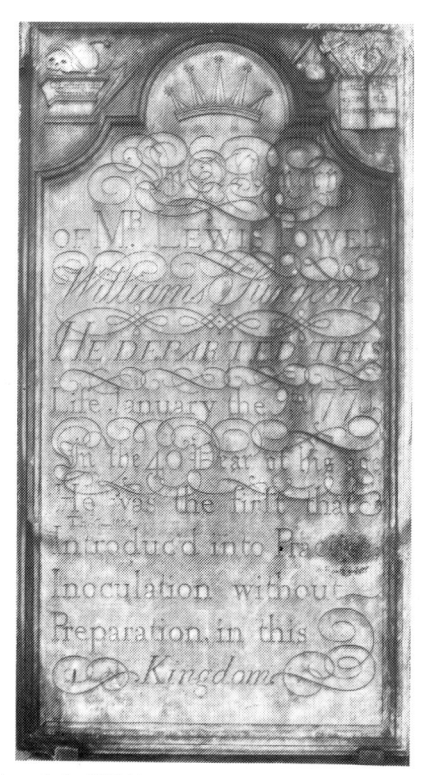

A medical "first" at Kibworth St. Wilfrid

Samuel Rouse (d.1775)
Market Harborough, St. Mary in Arden

amateur scientist of Market Harborough

Samuel Rouse was a talented mathematician, amateur astronomer and mechanic. He was a friend of William Whiston (q.v.) and Reverend William Ludlam (q.v.), and also a respected acquaintance of John Smeaton, builder of the third Eddystone lighthouse. Rouse is said to have been the first person to attempt to bring the bent-lever balance into use, although two other people obtained the patent. He lacked opportunities to use his talents and worked for most of his life as a draper in Market Harborough. In 1775 he died broken-hearted and penniless, and was buried at St. Mary in Arden.

His son Rowland Rouse (1739-1823) was one of Market Harborough's most eminent historians.

Joseph Nutt (1700-1775)
Hinckley, St. Mary

a Hinckley apothecary's innovatory schemes

Joseph Nutt tried to improve the land around Hinckley "like in ancient Egypt by the overflowings of the River Nile", but in this case by using water from the rivers of Leicestershire. His novel schemes involved washing water over the surface of Hinckley's roads. The idea was that the soft sand and mud which this flushed out went onto the land to improve the soil, whilst the residue of larger stony particles left behind made for harder and better road surfaces. He also recommended to the parish authorities that by using more stone and gravel in the construction of highways instead of sand dug from the roadside, substantial improvements could be achieved. However his innovatory ideas often met with considerable opposition, not least on the grounds of expense.

Nutt was equally well-known as one of the town's leading apothecaries and it is this aspect of his work which is commemorated on his gravestone in St. Mary's churchyard. It tells how for over fifty years he "assisted the poor and unfriendly with medicines and advice, without any other prospect of reward than that heartfelt satisfaction which must always accompany beneficent actions." His death in 1775 was greatly lamented both by friends and by those who he had freely helped. Charitable to the end, he bequeathed five large oak trees to the town to help provide a new school.

Dr William Watts (1725-1786)
Medbourne, St. Giles
(Also commemorated at Leicester, St. Martin)

founder of the Leicester Royal Infirmary

Leicester's Royal Infirmary owes its foundation to Dr Watts, a quiet man who pioneered the improvement of conditions for the sick and the poor.

He grew up at Danet's Hall in Leicester and after training for the medical profession, became one of the first physicians at the newly established Northampton Infirmary. Later he left to take Holy Orders and in 1762 returned to Leicestershire as curate of Medbourne. Inspired by what he had seen at Northampton Infirmary, he set about promoting a similar institution for Leicester. Despite considerable initial opposition, his scheme was eventually successful, and in 1771 the much needed Leicester Infirmary opened. The original site is still in use today and much of the first building still stands. Its original wrought-iron gates, which came from Quenby Hall, are now a short distance away in the gardens of Leicester's Newarke Houses Museum. Early facilities provided for some forty beds. Funding was by subscription, admission being at the recommendation of subscribers.

After the Infirmary's opening, Dr Watts withdrew into the background and his later life seems comparatively obscure. He was appointed curate of Narborough in 1774 but was in London at the time of his wife's death in 1783. She was buried at King's Norton and shortly afterwards he returned to Medbourne, where he lived until his own death, a few days before Christmas in 1786.

There are memorials to Dr Watts at Medbourne and Leicester. At St. Giles' Church Medbourne where he was buried, is a beautiful commemorative stained glass window given by the Friends of Leicester Royal Infirmary in 1946. Close by is a memorial tablet, a copy of which is in the nurses' chapel at the Infirmary. A medieval wooden stall in the chancel of St. Martin's Cathedral Leicester also bears his name.

Stained glass window at St. Giles Medbourne, showing Dr Watts holding a model of the Leicester Infirmary

Reverend William Ludlam (1717-1788)
Leicester, St. Mary de Castro

a mechanical genius

William Ludlam was a noted eighteenth century mathematician and astronomer celebrated for his mechanical genius. Born in Leicester the son of a local doctor, he distinguished himself both as a student and fellow of St. John's College, Cambridge where he later held the position of Linacre lecturer in physics. Highly regarded not only for his teaching abilities but also for his practical skills, he was one of three experts appointed by the government in 1765 to consider proposed solutions to the all-important longitude question. Three years later after accepting a college living, he retired to Leicester where for some twenty years he devoted himself to mechanics, astronomy, theology and writing. His prolific output included contributions to many contemporary journals as well as a standard Cambridge textbook. Many of his astronomical observations were made locally, Leicestershire's highest point at Bardon Hill being a favourite spot.

Ludlam died on 16th March 1788 and was buried at St. Mary de Castro, Leicester. Afterwards, his unusual collection of tools was sold off privately, whilst his models, machines, astronomical, optical and mathematical instruments, many of which he had made himself, were auctioned off at the Globe Tavern in London. According to Nichols, Ludlam's epitaph was intended to be:

"HERE RESTS A MAN, WHOM GENIUS GAVE TO SWAY
THROUGH THE BRIGHT COMPASS OF ETHEREAL DAY;
WHOSE BOUND, NOR TIME, NOR DISTANCE COULD CONTROUL,
BUT BORE HIM BOLDLY ON FROM POLE TO POLE,
PIERC'D THE DARK REGIONS OF ALL-COVERING NIGHT,
AND GAVE TO NEWTON'S SELF A CLEARER LIGHT."

There is no obvious trace of this inscription at St. Mary's today, although good eyesight should be able to pick his name out on the interestingly worded memorial to his son Thomas which hangs high up in the south aisle.

Robert Bakewell (1725-1795)
Dishley, All Saints

leading agriculturalist and pioneer stock breeder

Robert Bakewell was one of the greatest agricultural pioneers this country has ever known. A Leicestershire man by birth, he lived at Dishley Grange near Loughborough, where he experimented with scientific methods which were to revolutionise English agriculture.

Best remembered for his work on stock improvement, he altered the typical shape of English farm animals beyond recognition, more than doubling the average weight of sheep and cattle, often producing specimens "as fat as bears". His successes included the famous Leicestershire breed of sheep, as well as improvements to horses and long-horned cattle. These dramatic results were largely achieved through stock selection and selective breeding, methods which some of his more morally minded contemporaries disapproved of on incestuous grounds. He is also remembered for introducing the practice of hiring out stock for breeding. All his work was carefully recorded and a collection of preserved carcases and skeletons illustrating the results of his experiments was kept at Dishley for showing to the farm's many visitors. As an all-round farmer he was equally bold, experimenting with new feeding techniques, overwintering, direct reseeding, crop growing, dung collection and irrigation. Some of his ditches and waterways are still visible at Dishley and part of his farmland remains in agricultural use, although increasingly threatened by the rapidly encroaching outskirts of Loughborough.

Dishley Church where Bakewell was buried fell into ruin during the nineteenth century. For many years his gravestone lay hidden and forgotten beneath ivy, fallen roof timbers and broken masonry. Then in 1919, efforts to clear the debris by a group of former German prisoners of war who were working on Dishley Farm, revealed several tombstones in the chancel floor. One of these, although badly cracked was easily identified by a Mrs. Potter of the farm. On it she was able to read:

> "SACRED TO THE
> MEMORY OF
> ROBERT BAKEWELL,
> WHO DEPARTED THIS
> LIFE OCT. 1. 1795
> AGED 70 YEARS."

Curiously Dishley register contains no record of Bakewell's burial. The church ruins have since been restored and rededicated, and today Bakewell's stone lies behind the altar rails, its inscription repeated above on the more recently erected slate wall memorial.

Robert Bakewell's tombstone lies beyond the altar rail in the ruins of Dishley Church near Loughborough

Twentieth century wall plaque at Dishley Church commemorating Robert Bakewell

Dr Thomas Kirkland (1721-1798)
Ashby-de-la-Zouch, St. Helen

a Doctor's museum of curiosities at Ashby

Most eighteenth century towns boasted a celebrated doctor. In Ashby this was Dr Thomas Kirkland, an entertaining and gregarious local character of considerable medical abilities. He was also a lover of the arts and music. His most famous medical case concerned the death in 1760 of murder victim John Johnson (q.v.) in which he played a major role for the prosecution in obtaining the conviction of the fiery-tempered Laurence Shirley, 4th Earl Ferrers (q.v.). Afterwards the fatal bullet which had killed Johnson, and the silken hangman's rope by which the Earl subsequently perished, both found their way into the Doctor's museum of curiosities at Ashby where they joined pieces from Shakespeare's and Milton's mulberry trees; part of an Egyptian mummy; weapons from the Battles of Bosworth and Bunker's Hill; and many other curiosities. Dr Kirkland was also the author of a number of medical papers including one on the mysterious "Kink Cough".

He died in January 1798 and was interred near the chancel steps at St. Helen's, Ashby. His relatively plain marble wall memorial high up in the north aisle between the Adams Window and the north door was erected by his nephew. The distinguished scholar and cartographer John Prior (1729-1803) who was a friend of the doctor, is also commemorated on the same wall.

Thomas Barker (1722-1809)
Lyndon, St. Martin

a meticulous observer of the weather

Close to William Whiston's headstone at Lyndon (q.v.) is that of his grandson Thomas Barker. The now badly weathered inscription used to read:

> *"IN MEMORY OF THOMAS BARKER, ESQ.*
> *HE CONCLUDED A LONG AND MOST EXEMPLARY LIFE,*
> *DEC. 29, 1809, AGED 88 YEARS."*

Barker, although not so well known as Whiston, was one of the most important weather observers in this country during the eighteenth century. He lived at Lyndon Hall where for a long period he meticulously logged meteorological and climatic conditions. His observations were recorded in the Philosophical Transactions of the Royal Society and in his own journal. These have recently proved invaluable to the University of East Anglia in a research project aimed at compiling a detailed weather history of the eighteenth century. He also took a keen interest in astronomy, theology, vegetarianism and natural history. Gilbert White, the famous naturalist of Selborne was his brother-in-law.

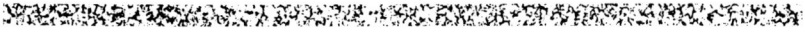

John Johnson (1732-1814)
Leicester, St. Martin

designer of the Jockey Club Rooms at Newmarket

The well-known sculptor John Bacon (1740-1799) left behind a large number of carvings both in this country and in Jamaica. His work includes busts of George III and Inigo Jones, statues of Henry VI and Samuel Johnson as well as figures for the Wedgewood and Derby Porcelain factories. He also carved a great many church monuments, one of which can be found on a wall in St. Dunstan's Chapel at Leicester Cathedral. It depicts Hope with an anchor and was carried out to the design of his friend and admirer John Johnson. Originally dedicated as a memorial to Johnson's parents, it has a further short inscription added at a later date to Johnson himself:

"IN MEMORY OF
JOHN JOHNSON, ARCHITECT.
(LATE OF THE PARISH OF ST. MARY-LE-BONE LONDON.)
SON OF THE ABOVE NAMED JOHN & FRANCES JOHNSON,
AND FOUNDER OF THE CONSANGUINITARIUM IN THIS TOWN."

John Johnson was a versatile, talented architect of considerable abilities. The County Rooms in Leicester, built initially as a hotel for racegoers is his best known surviving work locally. Other Leicester buildings such as his Consanguinitarium, theatre and gaol have long been demolished. Much of his working life was spent in the south of England, both on private commissions and in his official capacity as surveyor and architect for the County of Essex. The Shire Hall at Chelmsford was said to be his own favourite work. Elsewhere he designed churches, buildings, schools, stables and country houses, as well as the Jockey Club Rooms at Newmarket (since rebuilt). His varied interests extended to designing garden structures and landscapes, property specu-

49

lation, banking and experimental work on building materials. As an inventor he patented several ideas one of which was a method of preventing fires in buildings.

Johnson retired to Leicester where he died on 17th August 1814, and was buried with his parents at St. Martin's.

The Johnson memorial by John Bacon, Leicester St. Martin

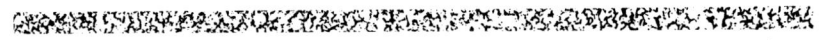

Samuel Deacon (1746-1816)
Barton-in-the-Beans, General Baptist Chapel

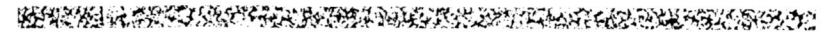

clockmaker and renowned Baptist preacher

Barton-in-the-Beans may be best known today for its unusual name, but during the late eighteenth and early nineteenth centuries it was noted both as an important centre for the General Baptist Church and as the home of Leicestershire's most famous family of clockmakers. Samuel Deacon junior who founded the clockmaking business was not only a mechanical genius but also renowned as a Baptist preacher throughout the Midlands.

Deacon spent his childhood in Ratby where he learnt knitting, spinning and reading. Later he was sent into farm service not far from London. He preferred studying to ploughing though, and frequently found himself in trouble with his master for supposedly neglecting his duties. A chance encounter however was to change his whole life. One evening in 1761 a friend of his employer who was travelling from Derbyshire to London was put up overnight at the farm. After supper Samuel was called on to provide the visitor with his pair of homemade wooden nutcrackers. The visitor was so impressed with the ingenuity of the implement that he afterwards arranged for Samuel to return to Leicestershire as an apprentice clockmaker to Joseph Donisthorpe of Normanton-le-Heath. Later Samuel obtained work in Leicester with clockmaker Thomas Lindley. Whilst there he also became acquainted with the Reverend William Ludlam (q.v.) from whom he learnt most about mechanics and clockmaking.

In 1771 Deacon set up his own business at Barton where he made everything from church, long case and musical clocks, to watches and barometers. His personal favourite was a musical clock made for the Reverend William Severn of Hinckley in 1790. It had a day indicator, a volume control and automatically played sixty-five different tunes. Every three hours as the music chimed, a mechanical band of violins, violincello, flute, vocalists and a boy and girl "all decently habited" would respectively play, beat time and dance to the music.

For forty years Deacon was also the highly popular minister of Barton's General Baptist Chapel, where today a wall tablet pays tribute to his worthiness. It also tells of his "ready wit...fluent utterance" and "striking aptness at appropriate metaphor". Other members of the family who carried on the clockmaking business after his death are commemorated in the burial ground outside the chapel. The last of the Deacons to make clocks at Barton was Thomas William Deacon (1892-1973), and when he moved from Barton in 1951 many items from the early days of the business were discovered in a workshop in the grounds of the house. These were subsequently acquired by Leicestershire Museums and are now on display at Leicester's Newarke Houses Museum.

Dr Robert Chessher (1750-1831)
Peckleton, St. Mary Magdalene.
(Also commemorated at Hinckley, St. Mary)

England's first orthopaedist

Dr Robert Chessher of Hinckley has recently received belated but deserved recognition as England's first orthopaedist. He pioneered the use of mechanical devices for treating spinal deformities and fractures, curing many people who would otherwise have remained crippled for life. His skills earned him a national reputation and at times he had up to two hundred people from all over the country on his books. Many took up temporary lodgings in the Hinckley area whilst being treated. Famous patients included William Wilberforce, Napoleon Bonaparte's niece, and George Canning's son. The Cannings briefly rented a house in Hinckley but disliked the town immensely and soon moved to neighbouring Burbage, occupying the building which today houses the Burbage and District Constitutional Club. Chessher also treated the poor, adjusting fees to suit means.

His inventions included a double inclined plane which was used for supporting fractured limbs, and a frame-like body brace known as "Chessher's Collar" which lifted the weight of the head off the spine, allowing the back to be held in the correct position.

When Chessher died, eight mourning coaches and four, and a long train of carriages accompanied the cortège to St. Mary's at Peckleton. His unusual convex horizontal tombstone lies in the eastern part of the churchyard. Inside the church is a highly attractive landscape memorial tablet, whilst a few miles away at St. Mary's Hinckley is a further tribute to his work on the chancel wall near the altar.

Attractive landscape memorial tablet to Robert Chessher, Peckleton St. Mary Magdalene

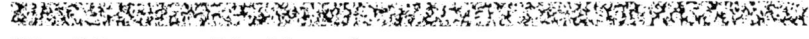

Sir Henry Halford (1766-1844)
Wistow, St. Wistan

royal physician who helped to identify King Charles I's remains

Sir Henry was born in Leicester under the name of Henry Vaughan. He took up a career in medicine and quickly reached the top of the profession. Regarded as one of the most successful and fashionable London doctors of his day, he had a long list of patients which included most of the royal family and many other celebrities such as Fox, Pitt and Canning. As royal physician, he successively served George III, George IV, William IV and Queen Victoria. George III much preferred him to any of the other "mad" doctors, rewarding his services with a baronetcy in 1809. At about the same time, Sir Henry inherited the Halford family estate at Wistow and changed his name from Vaughan to Halford. Constantly involved with royalty, Sir Henry became very much a courtier, acting not only as physician, but also as royal family confidant and go-between on delicate missions. A stickler for formality and propriety, the story goes that his first reaction upon seeing the lifeless body of Lord Liverpool, who had suffered a fatal cerebral haemorrhage, was to give "three profound formal bows". Such manners made Sir Henry an easy target for contemporary satirists. He was however regarded as a good practical physician, and from 1820 to 1844 was President of the Royal College of Physicians.

In 1813 Halford was summoned by the Prince Regent to examine an unidentified coffin which had been discovered during renovation work on the Royal Chapel at Windsor. Covered with a black velvet pall and lying close to the tomb of King Henry VIII, it was rumoured to be the "missing" coffin of King Charles I. Sir Henry's vivid account of the examination tells how the evidence left no doubt that it was indeed the body of the unfortunate Stuart monarch. Afterwards, when the coffin was resealed, some of the neck bones were not replaced and found their way into Sir Henry's possession. Stories circulated later alleging that the royal relic was being displayed to guests over the dinner table at Wistow Hall. During Queen Victoria's reign, the matter was brought to the attention of the Prince of Wales, who quickly saw to it that the royal remains were returned to their proper place. A lock of the King's hair, also removed in 1813, is reported to have been given to Sir Walter Scott as a present from Halford.

Sir Henry spent his later years at Wistow where his activities included restoration work on the church, as well as improvements to the hall and grounds. For a while he had a collection of exotic animals in the park, including two emus that were given to him by King George IV.

Sir Henry died in 1844, and was buried at St. Wistan's, Wistow. His memorial inside the church by R. Westmacott junior shows a doctor attending a sickbed, and is one of the finest in the county.

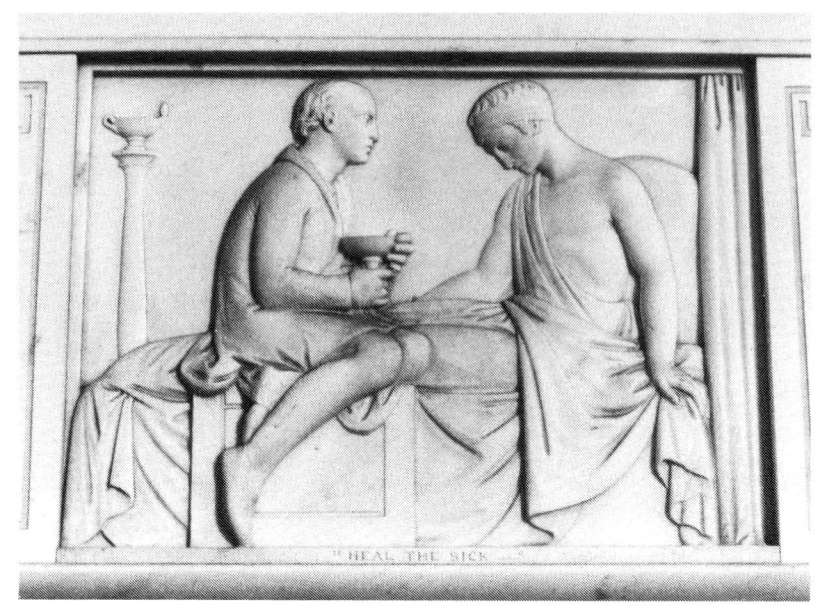

Richard Westmacott junior's outstanding memorial to royal physician Sir Henry Halford, Wistow St. Wistan

Reverend William Pearson (1767-1847)
South Kilworth, St. Nicholas

founder member of the Royal Astronomical Society

For over a quarter of a century from 1821 to 1847, the quiet rural Leicestershire village of South Kilworth was the home and living of William Pearson, a noted and important nineteenth century astronomer. He was a founder member and the first treasurer of the Royal Astronomical Society. In 1829 he won the Society's gold medal for his "Introduction to Practical Astronomy", a work which was acclaimed by the astronomer Sir John Herschel to be one of the most important and extensive books ever published on the subject. Pearson's other achievements included a ten year project which replotted the positions of over 500 stars. Many of his observations were made in a building which still stands just south of the Kilworth – Rugby Road. Although now a private home, the original octagonal shape of the observatory is still visible. Amongst the astronomical instruments he collected there were a three foot altazimuth originally constructed for St. Petersburg Academy of Sciences, and a large refracting lens which at the time was the largest of its kind in England.

South Kilworth not only had a very learned vicar in William Pearson, but also an extremely generous benefactor. He gave the village its first school, rebuilt part of St. Nicholas' Church and provided the organ and plate. He is commemorated inside the church by an attractive wall plaque decorated with a globe, telescope and book. Outside in the middle of the northern part of the churchyard, a prominent quatrefoil headstone surrounded by low railings marks the site of his grave.

A globe, telescope and book decorate astronomer William Pearson's memorial, South Kilworth St. Nicholas

Amelia Woodcock (d.1863)
Hambleton, St. Andrew

"The Wise Woman of Wing"

Today the most likely reason for a stranger to visit Wing is to see its mysterious turf maze. In the nineteenth century there was a further attraction, a local celebrity named Amelia Woodcock, better known as "The Wise Woman of Wing". She was a labourer's wife, who despite having no nursing or medical training, rapidly established a reputation for having the power to cure all manner of diseases, including cancer. Some believed her to have supernatural powers, others thought she was a witch.

As her fame spread, the villagers of Wing found themselves providing temporary lodgings for visitors from all over the country. The impression she made on people is vividly recorded in "Notes and Queries":

> "I shall not easily forget the impression produced by the woman's appearance and her surroundings. She was thin, bony, and weird-like; her countenance deep, dark and searching; her voice sharp, short, and decisive. On the fire a pot was boiling, over which she stood, and occasionally putting something in, repeated to herself words perfectly unintelligible to me. After a short time thus occupied she turned suddenly upon us, and said, 'I know what's the matter with you all . . . you're consumptive, and will all be dead in three years'. This reception was, to say the least, startling; but we held our peace; the woman and place awed us. A consultation followed, and soon ended; certain large bottles, or jars of mixture were brought home".

Quantity featured strongly in most of her prescriptions and meant that the local chemists had to keep her supplied with drugs by the cart-load. One "small" order ran:

> "Dear fren eye have sent you a small order if you think well to excep it 6 gallands of niter and a large bottle of dark mixture 1 galland of savaletta 1 galland of lavander 1 quart of oil of juneper and 6 pound of black plaster the same of red and 3 pound of gelap 3 of hilepica 6 bottles of quine."

In contrast to her reputation of curing others, Amelia Woodcock was barely middle-aged when she died, supposedly because of her "neglecting to take exercise, and to the habits that her confined life produced".

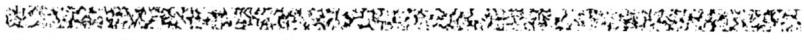

John Sydney Crossley (1812-1879)
Barrow-upon-Soar, Holy Trinity

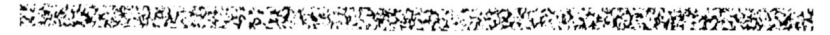

engineer of the Settle – Carlisle railway line

On a large stone cross in Barrow-upon-Soar churchyard is the name of John Sydney Crossley, the engineer under whose direction the railway line through Barrow was widened from two to four tracks. He has however a greater claim to fame, in connection with a railway line which few would dispute as England's most scenic route.

Crossley was born at Loughborough on Christmas day 1812 and was orphaned at the age of four. Christopher Staveley, a Leicester architect, acted as his guardian and later arranged for him to be apprenticed to his own son Edward Staveley, engineer of the Leicester Navigation Company. The facts surrounding Crossley's early life are less than clear, but it seems that following Edward Staveley's departure to America in 1833, Crossley took over as engineer of the canal company. During the next quarter of a century, he worked on various engineering and surveying projects including the Leicester and Swannington railway. For a while he was engaged by the Leicester Waterworks Company and in 1853 produced a report on the condition of the river Soar which included recommendations for preventing the frequent flooding of the western parts of Leicester. He also became a partner in one of the town's leading bookshops following his marriage to Agnes Combe, daughter of the bookseller Thomas Combe, in 1837.

In 1857 Crossley was appointed resident engineer for the Midland Railway Company, becoming Engineer-in-Chief the following year. As such he was responsible for a number of lines, his greatest achievement being the engineering of the 72¼ miles of the Settle and Carlisle railway. Cut through some of the most difficult terrain in the country, the line took six years to complete, eventually opening for main line passenger traffic on Monday 1st May 1876. Amongst the many outstanding structures on the line is the twelve span Smardale Viaduct north of Kirkby Stephen, 711 feet long and 130 feet high. Work on this was the final part of the difficult "No. 2" contract which went from Dent Head to Smardale and as it neared completion, the contractors invited Mrs Crossley to lay the viaduct's last stone. With appropriate ceremony, the massive stone block six feet in length was lowered into position bearing the inscription: " This last stone was laid by Agnes Crossley, June 8th, 1875". Her name is also on the monument in Barrow churchyard.

Crossley died at his home in Barrow on 10th June 1879. The house has since been demolished, but Crossley Close near the railway line is named after him. The lychgate at Holy Trinity is also erected to his memory.

Joseph Gordon (1836-1889)
Leicester, Welford Road Cemetery

designer of many European sewerage and drainage schemes

Joseph Gordon was a highly talented civil engineer. He designed sewerage and drainage systems for a number of large European, Scottish and English Cities. As Borough Surveyor of Leicester from 1880 to 1889 he tackled many of the town's appalling sanitary problems, greatly reducing the death rate in the long term. He was responsible for re-laying Leicester's sewers and also for the Beaumont Leys sewage irrigation farm, which at the time was the largest such scheme in England. In 1889 he left Leicester to take up the prestigious post of Chief Engineer to the new London County Council, but died a few weeks later on an omnibus at St. John's Wood. His funeral took place at Leicester Cemetery where his gravestone can be found along the southern perimeter path, not far from the University Road entrance.

Clement Stretton (1850-1915)
Leicester, Welford Road Cemetery

a leading promoter of railway safety

In an article about Clement Stretton published in 1893 it was claimed that he had probably done more for railway safety than "any other man breathing".

Born in Leicester the son of a former Mayor, he was articled as an engineer near Derby in 1866. He later returned to Leicester and in 1878 set up in business as a consulting engineer, specialising in railway engineering. For many years he enjoyed a high professional reputation, his expertise being sought after by both the government and the railway companies. Through investigating most of the major British railway accidents from 1869, he became a leading authority on railway safety, and many of his views on the subject were subsequently embodied in the Railway Act of 1889. His work was also greatly appreciated by railway employees throughout the country, and he became their national hero after his evidence on the Hexthorpe disaster saved the engine driver from going to prison for manslaughter.

In 1893 Stretton was appointed England's special representative to the railway department of the Chicago Exhibition. For this he prepared more than 1,500 photographs, books and papers, along with examples of early rail chairs weighing some ten tons. The collection was later dispersed to various museums in England. He was also the author of some 150 books and pamphlets, the best known of these being "Safe Railway Working", "Locomotive Development", and "History of the Midland Railway". His researches also formed the subject matter for a number of popular lectures which he delivered throughout the country.

He died at his home in Saxe Coburg (now Saxby) Street, Leicester early in 1915 and was buried in the Welford Road Cemetery.

3. Artists and musicians

Sir George Howland Beaumont
(1753-1827)
Coleorton, St. Mary

artist who helped found the National Gallery

The setting of St. Mary's Church Coleorton is one of the loveliest in Leicestershire. The building stands high on a hilltop adjacent to the beautiful wooded grounds of Coleorton Hall, about a mile from the village itself. Inside are a number of memorials to members of the Beaumont family who used to live at the hall. On the east wall of the south aisle is a simple Grecian-style tablet to Sir George Howland Beaumont who died in 1827 at the age of seventy-two. Its brief inscription reveals little else.

Sir George was in fact an outstanding patron of the arts and one of the best amateur landscape painters of his day. He gave his patronage and friendship to a great many artists including Constable, Cozens and Girtin, and was an early supporter of Landseer and Collins. Sir Joshua Reynolds was a close friend and a lifelong source of inspiration. Beaumont's greatest achievement was the leading part he played in establishing the National Gallery. He secured the Angerstein Collection for its foundation and added many outstanding works from his own collection by artists such as Claude, Poussin, Rembrandt, Rubens, Reynolds and Canaletto. He also bequeathed Michelangelo's famous "Tondo" to the Royal Academy. Sir George's own output was prolific – approximately 2,000 drawings and some 120 oils, examples of which are usually on display in Leicester at the Leicestershire Museum and Art Gallery on New Walk.

Coleorton Hall, which he renovated using profits from his Coleorton collieries, attracted many famous visitors including Wilberforce, Byron, Southey, Coleridge and Mrs Siddons. The winter garden at the hall was created by William Wordsworth, who also composed the verse on the Cenotaph to Reynolds that Sir George had erected in his grounds. The monument can still be seen there at the top of a tree-lined avenue. Close by are statues to Raphael and Michelangelo. A painting of the Cenotaph by Constable is in the National Gallery.

Another notable friend of the Beaumont family was Archbishop Halford of Canterbury who crowned Queen Victoria in 1838, and gave to Coleorton Church the chair used at the earlier coronation of William IV in 1831.

Sir George Beaumont's Cenotaph to Sir Joshua Reynolds in the grounds of Coleorton Hall. William Wordsworth wrote the verse

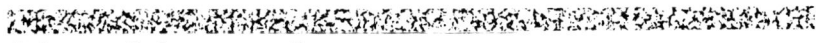

Mary Linwood (1755-1845)
Leicester, St. Margaret

celebrated Leicester embroiderer who became a household name

Mary Linwood, Leicestershire's most celebrated needlewoman, achieved international fame for her remarkable embroidered copies of well-known paintings. Her name became a household word and she was mentioned regularly in leading contemporary magazines and newspapers. For over fifty years there was a permanent exhibition of her work in London, described enthusiastically in guidebooks as one of "the sights of the city". Visitors to the exhibition claimed that her embroidered works resembled the original paintings so closely that it would be difficult to tell the two apart. Clever display techniques set the pictures off to their best advantage, whilst the use of gas lamps for the first time at such an exhibition not only enabled it to remain open after dark, but also added to the atmosphere.

She lived and worked in Leicester's Belgrave Gate, occupying a house known as the Priory (now demolished). At the height of her fame, strangers passing through Leicester broke their journeys and even missed coaches in the hope of seing her at work. The British royal family took an interest in her work, as did the Empress Catherine of Russia. She dined with Napoleon in Paris in 1803 and received the freedom of the city from him. Her charm, good looks and talents attracted many admirers although she never married. She also ran a private boarding school at the Priory. Her girls were a familiar sight around Leicester, as was her sedan chair, said to be one of the last in use in the country. As a patron of the arts she encouraged Leicester artist John Flower (q.v.), and is believed to have given Constable his first paid commission.

Perhaps anxious that posterity would forget her, she had her own epitaph erected during her lifetime. The inscription, which can be found on the memorial to her parents inside of St. Margaret's Church, Leicester reads:

"MARY THEIR DAUGHTER, DIED IN THE NINETEENTH CENTURY"

She died on 11th March, 1845. Many Leicester shops closed on the day of the funeral as a mark of respect, and a large crowd accompanied the procession from Belgrave Gate to St. Margaret's. Her remains were interred at the east end of the south aisle. Close by a tribute erected later by friends tells of her genius which "shed a lustre on her age, her country and her sex", and of her works which "are a splendid monument of art and perseverance." Both Linwood Lane and Mary Linwood School in Leicester are named in her honour.

The Priory, Belgrave Gate Leicester c.1845, home of Mary Linwood

William Gardiner (1770-1853)
Leicester, Welford Road Cemetery

self-confessed dilettante

When William Gardiner died, many felt that a part of Leicester's history died with him. Music lover, composer, performer, author, hosiery manufacturer and self-confessed dilettante, he had been a well-known character who for over half a century had played a leading role in the social and cultural life of the town. He further has the distinction of being regarded as the person who first introduced Beethoven's music into England, and some years later was honoured to take part in the ceremony of the unveiling of Beethoven's statue in Bonn. He also once wrote to Beethoven offering 100 guineas for an overture to "Judah" but the letter went astray, as did some stockings woven with music which he sent to Haydn.

Gardiner's compositions and arrangements include songs, duets, glees and an oratorio. A brief reference to his major work "Sacred Melodies" can be found on his plain upright headstone which stands in Leicester's Welford Road Cemetery, part way up the hill above the Welford Road entrance. Today however he is better known as the writer of "Music and Friends", a three volume autobiographical work which contains a wealth of fascinating local anecdotes, and makes compelling reading.

William Gardiner (by permission of Leicestershire Museums)

John Ferneley (1782-1860)
Thrussington, Holy Trinity
(Also commemorated at Melton Mowbray, St. Mary)

"The Landseer of the Midlands"

In Thrussington churchyard, to the left of the entrance gate and close to the north-west wall are two large similar mellow headstones. On the far side of one are the words:

"IN MEMORY OF JOHN FERNELEY (ANIMAL PAINTER) BORN AT THRUSSINGTON MAY 18TH 1782 DIED AT MELTON MOWBRAY JUNE 3RD 1860."

This simple epitaph, along with a similarly worded brass plaque in the chancel of St. Mary's Church at Melton Mowbray, commemorates the artist considered by many today to be the best of Leicestershire's sporting painters. His contemporaries also recognised his talents calling him "The Landseer of the Midlands".

Ferneley's early paintings were carried out on the wooden boards of waggons awaiting repair in his father's workshop. The 5th Duke of Rutland spotted his talents and arranged for him to study art in London under Ben Marshall. Marshall was a fellow Leicestershire man by birth, and one of the best known horse painters at that time. Later, after travelling around England and Ireland, Ferneley returned to Leicestershire and set up his studio at Melton Mowbray in the heart of England's most popular hunting country. One of his closest friends there was fellow artist Francis Grant (q.v.). The nobility and gentry were Ferneley's chief patrons and many nationally famous names can be found in the paintings of panoramic hunting scenes for which he is best known. Despite his increasing popularity, he kept his fees at the same levels. A horse portrait cost ten guineas and a medium size group of figures and horses between thirty and sixty guineas. Occasionally a larger canvas would go for one hundred guineas or more. Works which were partly painted by his son Claude were sold at lower rates. Today however, Ferneley's works command very high prices and examples of his paintings are usually on display in Leicester at the Leicestershire Museum and Art Gallery and at the Carnegie Museum in Melton Mowbray. Elgin Lodge where Ferneley lived at Melton was demolished amidst controversy in the early 1980's. Claude Ferneley's name appears on the roll of organists at St. Mary's Melton. Incidentally, one of his notable successors was Malcolm Sargent (later Sir) who is also listed there.

The Ferneley Family grave in Thrussington churchyard

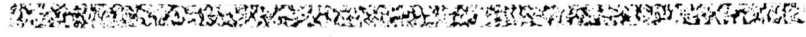

Edward Mammatt (1807-1860)
Ashby-de-la-Zouch Cemetery
(Also commemorated at Ashby, St. Helen)

musician and inventor

Set into a recess in the south wall of the Lady Chapel of St. Helen's at Ashby-de-la-Zouch, is a large arched monument decorated with musical angels. It commemorates Edward Mammatt, a talented amateur musician, composer and inventor. A remarkable man, who although being blind from the age of six, became a versatile lecturer and author on anatomy, astronomy, geology, electricity, sound, and pneumatics, as well as a successful manager of the Burton Brewery Company. He also invented a machine to assist the blind in writing, for which he received the Society of Arts gold medal, and admittance as a member. For forty years he was the organist at St. Helen's, where his musical compositions remained favourites with the congregation long after his death in April 1860. A stone memorial marks his grave in Ashby Cemetery.

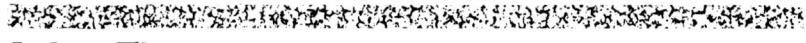

John Flower (1793-1861)
Leicester, Welford Road Cemetery

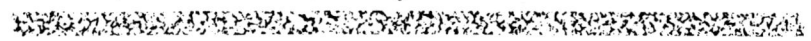

"The Leicester Artist"

Beneath the ivy clinging to a triple panelled Ketton stone monument in Leicester's Welford Road Cemetery, it is just possible to make out the name of John Flower. Referred to by his contemporaries as "The Leicester Artist", Flower's drawing skills were, and still are, highly thought of. William Gardiner (q.v.) considered him a genius, being a shining example of what "ardour, diligence, and good sense can achieve under circumstances by no means propitious".

Flower was born in Leicester and initially apprenticed as a frameworkknitter. His artistic talents were noticed and encouraged by Dr Alexander of Danet's Hall, and later with help from Mary Linwood (q.v.), he went to London to study art under the painter Peter de Wint. On returning to Leicester, he established himself as a talented artist and drawing master. Today his many drawings of Leicestershire provide a unique visual record of the area in the early nineteenth century. "Views of Ancient Buildings in the Town and County of Leicester" printed in 1826 contains some of the best known examples of his work. Many of his original sketches and drawings survive, and both Leicestershire Libraries and Leicestershire Museums have good collections of his work.

His house at 100, Regent Road Leicester still stands, the initials JF and the date 1851 visible on the front of the building. From there, a short walk along University Road leads to the Welford Road Cemetery where his monument will be found in the non-consecrated section not far from that to Thomas Cook (q.v.).

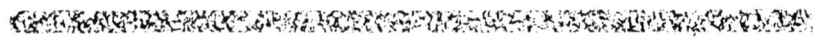

Sir Francis Grant (1803-1878)
Melton Mowbray, St. Mary's Close Church of England Cemetery
(Also commemorated at St. Mary's Church)

President of the Royal Academy who preferred Melton to St Paul's

Francis Grant was one of the most fashionable portrait painters of his day. Born in Scotland, the younger son of a wealthy Scottish laird, he first started painting as an enthusiastic amateur. After spending his inheritance by an early age and failing to make a career at the Bar, he decided to capitalise on his artistic talents and turn professional. Good living and field sports occupied much of the rest of his time. Hunting scenes featured prominently in his early paintings with his sporting friends providing a ready market. Later he concentrated on portraiture, his flattering style and personality attracting the patronage of many of the nobility, gentry and celebrities of the day. These included Queen Victoria, Melbourne, Disraeli, Palmerston and Macaulay. Like many of England's hunting fraternity, Grant was drawn to Melton Mowbray, where for a number of years during the season, he lived at a house known as "The Lodge".

In 1866 he was elected President of the Royal Academy, a position which he held until his death in 1878. The "Illustrated London News" welcomed the appointment, considering it an advantage to have as head of the painting profession, not only an able painter but also a "thoroughly manly, honest and courteous British gentleman". It was a post which also brought to its holder the privilege of being buried at St. Paul's Cathedral, London, an honour which Sir Francis did not take advantage of, preferring Melton instead.

His funeral was one of the most notable ever witnessed in Melton. On the day, a considerable number of Academians arrived from London by train, travelling in a special saloon carriage attached to the 12.55 from Leicester. They were joined at St. Mary's Church by friends, relatives and over two hundred local tradesmen. Businesses were temporarily closed and even the market stalls were covered over. Inside the church, the pulpit and chancel were draped in black. The Archbishop of York and the vicar of Melton jointly took the service. Afterwards, the procession made its way through the densely packed streets to the Church of England burial ground near King Street. The "Leicester Chronicle" found it difficult to understand why the cemetery had been chosen claiming that:

> "were it not for the gravestones that are to be seen the place would be taken for the stockyard of a farmhouse rather than a portion of "God's Acre"... What the members of the Royal Academy present at the funeral thought of the surroundings of the tomb of their chief we dare not pretend to say..."

However, the "Leicester Journal" reported that the cemetery had undergone a timely and much needed transformation at the expense of the friends of the deceased! Today it is an open park area. Many of the gravestones have been moved and either placed upright around its edge or laid flat as paving. Sir Francis' stone however, along with two other monuments, remains prominently placed near the centre, passed daily by those who use the path as a cut through between Norman Street and King Street.

Inside St. Mary's Church, there are several plaques in the vestry to members of the Grant family. Sir Francis himself is commemorated by a stained glass window which includes two haloed figures, one with an artist's palette, the other painting at an easel.

Only Sir Francis Grant's monument and two others still stand in the middle of St. Mary's Close Melton Mowbray

Anselm Baker (1833-1885)
Mount St. Bernard Abbey

"The Herald Monk"

Anselm Baker was one of the most distinguished heraldic artists of recent times. Known as "The Herald Monk", his artistic talents were unequalled in this country. His skills were widely acknowledged, not least by the College of Arms, and his work greatly sought after.

A native of Birmingham, he first acquired a knowledge of drawing and painting whilst working at Hardman's studios, a firm famous for its stained glass manufacture. In 1856 he came to Mount St. Bernard Abbey in Leicestershire where he lived and worked as a lay brother until his death in 1885.

The Abbey has a fine collection of his work including the beautiful and unique "Liber Vitae" (a record of the Abbey's benefactors illustrated with their arms and patron saints), its colours as fresh and bright today as when first painted. His highly regarded "Armorial Bearings of the English Cardinals" is cared for by the College of Arms. Amongst his published work are many of the illustrations in Foster's 1880 "Peerage". He also accomplished a number of mural paintings in the Midlands including that in the Infirmary Chapel at Mount St. Bernard. His heraldic style is particularly interesting in that it dispenses with the black outlines customarily used on coats of arms.

His death at the age of fifty-two on 11th February 1885 came as a great blow to the community and to his friends and admirers. He was buried in the community cemetery at Mount St. Bernard. In accordance with Cistercian practice, his body was interred without a coffin, dressed in the full habit of the order, with his face towards the east. Today his grave is marked by a simple metal cross about three feet high and which bears the name "Anselm".

4. Local characters

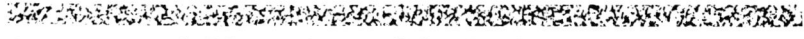

Reverend Humfrey Michel (c.1650-1722)
Blaston, St. Giles

in the rector's bad books

Whilst many parsons have had cause for concern over the behaviour of their parishioners, few have recorded their criticism in the way that Humfrey Michel did. Described as one of the strangest men who ever took Holy Orders, he was for almost half a century the despairing and often controversial rector of Blaston and Horninghold. Unknown to most of his parishioners he kept highly critical records of their conduct. His main targets were the "God-Robbers" who did not pay him their tithes; the "barn-goers" or nonconformists; those who did not take the sacrament, and all those who he considered were defrauding him by being buried or married in another parish:

> "John Muggleston, Repr. of St. Giles Parish in Blaston was buryed at Medbourn Aug 5 1715, he never received the sacrament of the Lords supper as I remember in 30 years time. And he that I should not officiate, I suppose first stole my bell rope, then my bell clapper and then the Bell . . .And that I should not Christen my child at church, he, I supposed all be-dung'd ye church-key-hole!"

> "1711 . . . a clandestin marriage. Mr John Clough locked the Church door so nobody could come and see em marry'd."

> "Francis Wells widow, . . . having not (as I remember) received the sacramental body & blood of Christ, twice in about 40 years by me, nor ever pay'd the Easter offerings (wch were also the Impious omission of her Husband) was buryed (they say) at Hallaton . . . Aug 10 1719."

His family often fared little better:

> April 27 1708: "My daughter so impudent she sent me a patched shirt, and her brother the whole one."

Witches and witchcraft also came under his attack as did the murderers of King Charles I.

Recording the death of his first wife in 1707, he wrote of her departure out of "ye miseries of this naughty world". Three years later at the age of sixty he remarried, commenting "Youth & Age ye best match still". His youthful wife bore him several sons, the last when he was nearly seventy. Not long afterwards his own death was entered in the registers when in November 1722 he was buried beneath the altar of St. Giles' at Blaston.

Thomas Bugg (d.1727)
Stathern, St. Guthlac

a drinking champion

Stathern parish register for 1727 contains an unusual entry in Latin concerning the burial of Thomas Bugg on 4th March that year. Such was Bugg's "fame", that the recorder considered it necessary to mention the deceased's capacity for drinking, in particular, his performance of a feat which seems to have been a kind of eighteenth century version of the "yard of ale". Bugg regularly drank six pints of ale in one go, using a special jug, which as the register says "vulgo dictum Buggs Pint". The vessel used to be preserved at Belvoir Castle.

By the time the poet George Crabbe (q.v. Sarah Crabbe) was living in the Vale, Bugg's name had passed into the folk history of the area. Crabbe also liked a drink and probably learned of Bugg and his reputation at one of the local inns. Afterwards he included the characters of both Bugg and the landlord in his poem "The Parish Register". In this, Andrew Collett, the blind, fat landlord of the Old Crown Inn, speaks in praise of former customers who enjoyed their ale, saying:

> "One, in three draughts, three mugs of ale took down,
> As mugs were then – the champion of the Crown."

Sir John Danvers (1723-1796)
Swithland, St. Leonard

country squire who saw red

Sir John Danvers, the son of Sir Joseph Danvers (q.v.) was another remarkable member of the family. With a mania for the colour red, not only did he paint his own house and stables red, but also every door, window-shutter, and gatepost in Swithland and Mountsorrel. He also favoured red for his own dress, which, when worn with black, was said to make him look like the Jack of Spades. Sir John lived at Swithland Hall and flew a flag from the highest point on the building whenever he was in residence. Another eccentricity was his insistence that no coal should be used in the hall, and thus in every corner of the building vast quantities of firewood were stockpiled.

It was this same Sir John, who having taken a fancy to the old market cross at Mountsorrel and removed it to the grounds of Swithland Hall, provided the village with its distinctive domed rotunda as a replacement. Mountsorrel was also the usual location for Sir John's annual Mowdebush Court. On the appointed day each year, his lawyer and steward would climb the Mowdebush Hill, where after a short ceremony, they would dig up a piece of turf which would be carried back to the house where the court was being held.

Anxious to perpetuate his memory as a lover of both the constitution and Protestantism, Sir John wrote his own epitaph to this effect. He had it erected during his lifetime, wording it to allow for his death "about the 18th century", anticipating that his remains would be "deposited under the small blue stone at the foot of the monument".

He died on 21st September 1796, and after lying in state at the Crown Inn at Leicester "surmounted by a magnificent plumage, decorated with escutcheons and all the paraphernalia of funeral pomp" was interred at St. Leonard's, Swithland. Of the many impressive memorials to the Danvers family inside the church, Sir John's is the large one now situated in the middle of the north wall.

Mountsorrel's rotunda replaces an earlier market cross which the eccentric Sir John Danvers removed to Swithland Hall

Sampson Cartwright (c.1770-1854)
Rothley, St. Mary and St. John the Baptist

Rothley native who was Nelson's errand boy

For many years, Rothley born ex-army veteran Sampson Cartwright was one of Belgrave Gate's best known inhabitants. Tales of his daring soldierly exploits and miraculous escapes whilst serving as a foot soldier in the Peninsular War, made him something of a living legend. Broad shouldered, brawny and capable of bearing any amount of fatigue, his courage was described as "bulldog" in the highest degree. He loved danger and excitement. In later years he was always ready to relate his soldiering adventures and seemingly unbelievable tales whenever a chance arose. He also proudly reminisced about the time when he was Admiral Nelson's errand boy.

Discharged from the army shortly before Waterloo, he came and settled in Leicester, making and selling trunks and band-boxes. He hated radicals, rioters and reformers, and was always on hand to offer his services to the local constabulary.

In his mid-sixties, his thoughts turned to having his coffin prepared and about 1838 he ordered one, giving instructions that it be painted blue, declaring that he had lived all his life blue and that he would die blue. The local liberal newspaper the "Leicester Chronicle" picked up the story and ran it under the disrespectful headline "Blue for ever", mentioning that the coffin contained several shelves so it could be used as a corner cupboard until needed. Infuriated, Sampson leapt into action, threatening to blow up the newspaper's premises and shoot the proprietors. However, the "Chronicle" survived, and following Sampson's death considerably later, it printed a respectful obituary entitled "Death of a Veteran". Sampson was buried in his blue coffin as he had wished, with four staunch Tory acquaintances acting as bearers. His grave lies in Rothley churchyard but the site is presently unmarked.

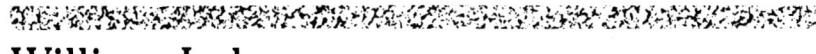

William Lole (d.1874)
Swepstone?

"The Old Hermit of Newton Burgoland"

One of the most colourful and eccentric characters to live in the west of the county was William Lole the self-styled "Old Hermit of Newton Burgoland". Long-bearded and of venerable appearance, he looked more like a dandy than a hermit, and led a life that was far from that of a recluse. He had a mania for symbols, emblems and mottoes which was apparent not only in his dress but also at his home.

He had over twenty numbered and oddly-named hats of his own design, to each of which he gave an emblem or motto. His number five hat was the "Bellows", adorned with the motto "Blow the flames of freedom with God's word of truth". Number seven was the "Helmet", inscribed "Will fight for the birthright of conscience, love, life, property, and national independence". Hat number one called "Odd Fellows" and bearing the motto "Without money, without friends, without credit", was probably sported when he felt down on his luck. Others were called the "Patent Tea-pot", the "Wash-basin of Reform", and the "Bee-hive". He also had twelve highly individual "suits", each of which was similarly given a name and intended to be symbolic. "Odd Fellows" was a loose fitting garment of white linen, bound around the waist with a white girdle buckled at the front, and with a heart-shaped badge bearing the words "Liberty of Conscience" on the top left hand side. "Foresters" was a kind of frock-coat made of soft brown leather embroidered with braid, with white buttons down the front and a white buckled girdle around the waist. The accompanying hat had black and white stripes and was shaped like a turban. There was also "Military" which resembled an antique military costume. All a far cry from the popular sackcloth and ashes image of other hermits.

The garden of his cottage at Newtown Burgoland was also eccentric, containing all sorts of peculiar symbolic devices and statues. In the passage leading into the garden were three seats of "Self Inquiry" each inscribed with a question: "Am I a hypocrite?", "Am I vile?", "Am I a Christian?". The trees, flowers and shrubs were all symbolically arranged. There were also effigies of the apostles and mounds covered with flowers to represent the graves of the Reformers. Even the garden implements bore names and emblems such as "Conjugal bliss", "The Hermit's coat of arms" and "Gossips' Court". In the middle stood a makeshift pulpit consisting of a large tub and desk from which he harangued visitors. In summer the garden was opened for teas, visitors being charged according to their circumstances. With few other sources of income, however, he became extremely poor, and spent his latter years thankful for any assistance which did not require him to give up his garden. His house no longer stands, having been replaced by another earlier this century.

Lole died at Newton Burgoland and is believed to have been buried at Swepstone. Interestingly his death certificate gives his occupation as "formerly a Bookbinder", a business which he appears to have carried out in his earlier years near the old Exchange in Leicester.

"The Old Hermit of Newton Burgoland" in one of his many outfits

John William Stephens (1861-1908)
Leicester, Welford Road Cemetery

"The Laughing Policeman"

At 24 stone 3 lbs, Leicester's "Tubby" Stephens once held the record for being England's heaviest policeman. Witty, jovial and good-humoured, he was one of the best loved and most popular "bobbies" the town has ever had.

Tubby's fame spread far beyond Leicester. He became the subject of picture postcards and cartoons, and is reputed to have provided the inspiration for the song "The Laughing Policeman". Visiting theatrical performers were keen to be photographed with him, and away football supporters used to make it part of their day to find him for a bit of well meant fun. He kept good order though, his size being a ready asset to sort out any real trouble.

P.C. Stephens (by permission of the Leicester Mercury)

Tubby died at the comparatively early age of forty-eight, having just completed twenty-two years with the Leicester Force. The love and respect he had earned from both his colleagues and the public was evident at his funeral. Press reports tell of dense crowds lining the whole of the funeral route from his house in Cobden Street, past the Clock Tower to Horsefair Street and Market Street and down the Welford Road to the Cemetery. An estimated 10,000 people turned out to pay their last respects. Amongst the many tributes was this one from a colleague:

> "Draw down the blinds till the funeral train goes past
> Carrying a hero gone to rest at last.
> Thousands knew him, and hundreds say
> Kindness gained him the tears shed today.
> His work done well for his King and Queen,
> Policeman and soldier who had foreign service seen,
> Marching and fighting 'neath a burning sun
> While Zulus fell before the Gatling gun.
> No fancy slab or stone needs 'poor old Joe',
> Well known the place where a good man lies low;
> Let the grass grow green, and flowers the ground possess,
> By the grave where lies the late P.C.J.S."

As the verse suggests, no monument presently stands to mark Tubby's grave. A grand processional march, "The Pride of the Force", by Leicester composer Lawrence Wright, was later dedicated to his memory.

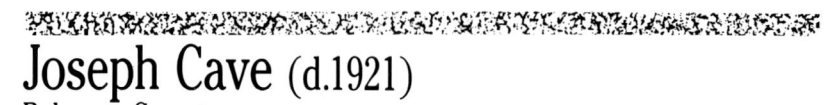

Joseph Cave (d.1921)
Belgrave Cemetery

Belgrave resident who sang in his grave

Mr. Joseph Cave of Victoria Road, Belgrave was a man who did not like doing things in a hurry, so in order to avoid the "hurry up" which usually accompanied funeral arrangements, he had his own grave and monument prepared well in advance. As the workmen cut the soil, Jo calmly watched from a seat in the cemetery, and on its completion, astonished the workmen by descending to the bottom for a smoke, a chat and a rendition of the song "Poor Old Joe". Afterwards the grave lay empty for some nine years, its elaborate uninscribed monument providing a puzzle for the curious visitor to Belgrave Cemetery. Shortly after Jo's death on 6th August 1921, the "Illustrated Leicester Chronicle" revealed the solution to the mystery by publishing his picture and story on the front page under the heading "A Belgrave resident who sang in his grave".

At over seven feet high, Jo's monument is one of the larger memorials in the cemetery, and can be found part way up the hill along the northern perimeter path.

Jimmy (James) Hawker (1836-1921)
Oadby Cemetery

a celebrated Midlands poacher

In the northern part of Oadby Cemetery is a small gravestone with the intriguing epitaph:

"I WILL POACH TILL I DIE."

It commemorates Jimmy Hawker, one of the most celebrated poachers in the Midlands. He lived in the days when poaching was considered an extremely serious offence, punishable by heavy fines, imprisonment and penal servitude:

"The mid 1840's were wretched times. Sheepstealing, highway robbery and burglary were common. It was not safe to go out after dark. If a man stole a sheep he had 14 years transportation. If hunger made a man go into the woods to get a pheasant, he too would get fourteen years. Two men in Oadby had 14 years – Jack Baurn, Bill Devonport – for attempting to take pheasants in Tugley Wood, in 1847." ("A Victorian Poacher").

Brought up in a very poor family at Daventry and undeterred by the penalties, Jimmy took up poaching as a teenager. Originally out of necessity, it later got "into his blood", becoming a way of life, even when he had regular work. For a while he tried the army, but deserted, realising that he could never be trained to kill peasants, although pheasants were another matter altogether! For most of his life, he lived in Northamptonshire and Leicestershire, taking various jobs and moving on as necessitated by periodic brushes with the law and gamekeepers. He felt strongly about the plight of the working classes, despising the rich who fed their pheasants hard-boiled eggs whilst the poor starved. He felt strongly about how one class could shoot game in the name of sport, but if the other did it out of necessity, they would be taken for breaking the law.

For the last thirty years of his life he settled with his family at Oadby, where despite his outdoor activities, he became a well liked and almost respectable member of the community. Noted for his common sense, charm, and liveliness, he found himself elected to the School Board in 1893. In the following year, as one of Oadby's first eight parish councillors, he took his place alongside those on whose land he still poached. Above all he remained proud to be a poacher, and lived up to his oft-repeated claim that he would poach 'til he died.

On 7th August 1921 Jimmy was found lying dead at the junction of Stoughton Road and New Lane. Officially, the cause of death was a heart attack. Unofficially, locals preferred the rumour that he had been shot. For many years afterwards his grave in Oadby Cemetery lay unmarked, until the Emma Theatre Company, whilst performing a stage version of his life, managed to raise sufficient money for a headstone. It was unveiled in May 1981 by Jimmy's great grand-daughter, Marjorie Briggs.

Jimmy's own interesting and highly readable account of his life, written when he was about seventy, was published later under the title "A Victorian Poacher". David Sneath and Barry Lount recently helped secure Jimmy's original manuscript for Leicestershire Record Office.

Memorial to poacher Jimmy Hawker, Oadby Cemetery

William H. Friswell (1872-1939)
Leicester, Gilroes Cemetery

"The Colonel"

The death of William H. Friswell in 1939 deprived Leicester of one of its most well-known characters. Known to thousands as "The Colonel" he made his mark as a super sandwich-board man!

Originally a native of Hinckley, he later moved to Leicester where for many years he was to be seen parading along the town's streets with his characteristic top hat, ribboned cane and sandwich-boards. Reported to have twenty changes of costume, he took immense pains to rehearse, turning the job of sandwich-board man into a true art. For a while he was the City mascot and in the Pageant of Leicester parade of famous local characters in 1932, was the only character there representing himself. He also once gave a memorable winning performance in a "Dunmow Flitch" contest held at Leicester's Corn Exchange. As England's "Number One Advertiser", he publicised hundreds of businesses, with his act being much in demand in the North of England and at the seaside, as well as in Leicester.

Early in November 1939, the "Leicester Mercury" reported the Colonel to be seriously ill. He died a few days later and on the day of his funeral scores of people crowded into Eaton Street where he had lived, to witness the procession leave for Gilroes Cemetery.

His grave is presently unmarked.

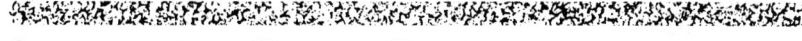

Christopher Risley Perkins (d.1957)
Lubenham, All Saints

known to the children of Market Harborough as Father Christmas

The death of Christopher Risley Perkins was reported in the "Leicester Evening Mail" under the headline "Harborough Man of Mystery dies". Described as Harborough's most eccentric figure, he was known for miles around. Easily recognisable by his long flowing white hair and beard, he wore unconventional dress and usually carried a walking stick. He lived in a large house on the Coventry Road in Market Harborough surrounded by numerous cats, and despite coming from a wealthy family, followed a very simple lifestyle spending much time alone with his books. Periodically he would take the train to Leicester for the day and is reported to have been in the habit of stopping strangers in the street for long discussions on politics. He is commemorated in Lubenham churchyard.

5. Industrialists, benefactors and reformers

John Wycliffe (c.1320-1384)
Originally buried Lutterworth, St. Mary

"The Morning Star of the Reformation"

Close to the bridge over the River Swift in Lutterworth is the site where one night in 1428 the disinterred remains of the famous reformer John Wycliffe were publicly burnt and his ashes cast into the water. This was a political and religious act of desecration, carried out in accordance with an edict from the Council of Constance, by authorities anxious to stop the spread of his heretical ideas.

Up the hill, back towards the centre of Lutterworth is the Church of St. Mary. Less than half a century earlier in 1382, Wycliffe had arrived there as rector, having been banned from preaching and teaching at Oxford because of his controversial doctrinal views. By then he was well-known as an outspoken critic of the established church, who considered that only radical reform would put things right. Amongst his beliefs was a principle that everyone should have access to the scriptures in a language they could understand. With this end in mind he set about producing the first common English translation of the whole of the Bible. This, his greatest work, was according to tradition carried out at Lutterworth.

Wycliffe died at Lutterworth on the last day of 1384 and his remains lay interred in the chancel until being rudely disturbed in 1428. Such efforts however failed to prevent the spread of his teachings, and through people like Luther, his ideas had a major influence on the Protestant Reformation. Wycliffe's followers became known as Lollards, who incidentally saw little need for consecrated burial grounds.

The nineteenth century white marble Wycliffe Memorial which today is the most prominent feature of St. Mary's south aisle at Lutterworth, is the work of the celebrated sculptor, Richard Westmacott junior. Originally it hung on a north wall of the chancel, but had to be moved when the north aisle was extended during the Gilbert Scott restoration. Too large for its new position, the lower portion was removed and subsequently re-used for the pulpit of Glenfield Methodist Church. Various relics which may have associations with the great reformer are also on display inside the church.

Richard Westmacott junior's monument to John Wycliffe, Lutterworth St. Mary

Archdeacon Robert Johnson (1540/1-1625)
North Luffenham, St. John the Baptist

controversial Puritan divine and local benefactor

On the southern wall of the chancel of St. John the Baptist, North Luffenham, is a small black-lettered bronze plaque to former rector and benefactor, Robert Johnson. Part of its lengthy Old English inscription runs:

"HE ERECTED A FAIRE FREE GRAMMAR SCHOOLE IN OKEHAM,
HE ERECTED A FAIRE FREE GRAMMAR SCHOOLE IN UPPINGHAM,
HE APPOINTED TO EACH OF HIS SCHOOLES A SCHOOLMASTER AND AN USHER,
HE ERECTED THE HOSPITALLE OF CHRISTE IN OKEHAM,
HE ERECTED THE HOSPITALLE OF CHRISTE IN UPPINGHAM."

The two "grammar schooles" referred to are of course the present day Oakham and Uppingham independent schools, where both the original sixteenth century buildings are still visible. Neither of Johnson's "hospitalles" still stand, but each town has a home for the elderly endowed from the original foundation.

Johnson himself was educated at Cambridge. Afterwards he was ordained as Deacon of Peterborough, and barely two years later achieved something of a coup by being appointed Chaplain to Sir Nicholas Bacon, Queen Elizabeth's Lord Keeper of the Great Seal. Other offices and benefices followed. These included the Archdeaconry of Leicester and the rectory of North Luffenham. Life at Luffenham was not without its problems, and Johnson had to contend with people boycotting his services because of his extreme Puritan views, and also with lengthy lawsuits over tithes.

His grandson Isaac, an emigrant to the New World, was one of the committee which chose to name Boston in America after the Lincolnshire town.

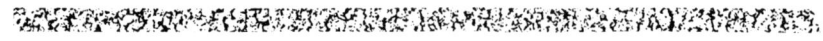

Reverend John Bold (1679-1751)
Stoney Stanton, St. Michael

a model clergyman

One of the most noticeable gravestones near the east gate of St. Michael's churchyard is the Reverend John Bold's. Situated at the foot of the church wall, it has an unusual headstone consisting of two separate slates. The top slate bears a large lettered tribute:

> "LET ME DIE THE DEATH OF THE RIGHTEOUS
> AND LET MY LAST END BE LIKE HIS."

and was added by the Reverend Robert Nickolls, a later minister whose own headstone is alongside.

Bold, a saintly and ascetic village pastor, has gone down in history as Leicestershire's "Model Clergyman". For almost half a century he served as curate in charge to an absentee vicar at Stoney Stanton, living a life of frugality, self-denial, piety and charity. He attentively watched over his parishioners, managing single-handed to almost eliminate crime in the parish.

> "His daily fare consisted of watergruel for his breakfast; a plate from the farmer's table, with whom he boarded, supplied his dinner; after dinner, one half pint of ale, of his own brewing, was his only luxury; he took no tea, and his supper was upon milk pottage (porridge). With this slender fare his frame was supported under the labour of his various parochial duties... He visited all his parishioners, exhorting, reproving, consoling, instructing them. And the effect of his instructions has been visible... in the piety, the probity, sobriety, and industry of those who were brought up under him." (John Nichols)

When the tenor bell was added to St. Michael's ring in 1898 it was inscribed: "IN MEMORY OF THE REV. JOHN BOLD OF 1751. WOE IS UNTO ME IF I PREACH NOT THE GOSPEL."

Alderman Gabriel Newton (1683-1762)
Leicester, All Saints

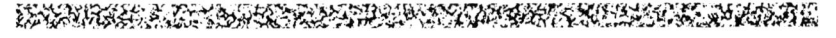

a crusty eccentric

The likenesses of four of Leicester's best known benefactors are carved on the Clock Tower. The stern faced, robed figure with a book in his hand is Alderman Gabriel Newton, a former Lord Mayor of Leicester who was a jersey comber by trade and one-time landlord of the Horse and Trumpet Inn. A pious, quarrelsome and "crusty but kindly eccentric", his greatest contribution was in the field of education, when over 200 years ago, he founded the school which still bears his name. Not far from the Clock Tower in the Sanctuary of Leicester Cathedral is a splendid large rococo wall memorial dedicated to Alderman Newton's only son George. Its inscription helps explain the story. It tells how George's early death caused his disconsolate and grieving father to not only erect the monument, but also to use a large part of his wealth to help provide much needed educational facilities for poorer children of the town. Above the inscription is an oval panel portraying a group of angelic boys at their lessons.

Newton's first school was connected with St. Martin's, lessons being held in the church. However, an undignified fight between Newton and the parish clerk seems to have been responsible for closing the school down. Undeterred, Newton persevered and some twenty years after his death, his plans reached fruition. Originally situated near the Jewry Wall and known as the Green Coat School, its pupils wore a distinctive uniform of a three-quarter length green coat with scarlet facings, waistcoat, knee-breeches, shirt, grey stockings and cap. Information about the school's subsequent rebuilding and enlargement, along with details of other bequests, can be found on Alderman Newton's own monument in All Saints' churchyard in Highcross Street. Pupils from the school have helped to take care of the monument, and there is a further memorial to him inside the church. The present day Alderman Newton's School is on Glenfield Road and has a roll of some 900 pupils.

Alderman Newton's figure on the Clock Tower, Leicester

Reverend William Hanbury (1725-1778)
Church Langton, St. Peter

a university at Church Langton?

Around the middle of the eighteenth century travellers between Gumley and the Langtons could not have failed to notice the large numbers of trees recently planted in the area. These plantations were part of an extraordinary scheme dreamed up by the Reverend William Hanbury.

Hanbury, who was rector of Church Langton from 1753 to 1778, was both a horticultural expert and a supreme optimist. He planned to sell the wood from these plantations when it was mature, and use the profits to turn the Langtons into a major educational and cultural centre. His proposals included establishing a collegiate foundation which would provide teaching and living accommodation for professors and scholars of Latin, Greek, music, botany, mathematics, antiquity and poetry. There was to be a "Temple of Religion and Virtue", a public library, an art gallery, an observatory and a printing press, with a magnificent new high-spired gothic cathedral at the centre of the complex. Further plans provided for a hospital and school.

As part of his promotional campaign Hanbury also launched an annual series of fund-raising concerts. The first was a very grand affair, the like of which had probably never before or since been witnessed in the Langtons. No expense was spared as galleries were erected in the church, a full London orchestra was hired, and a sumptuous banquet with cold dishes and ham pies a yard in diameter was provided! Hundreds of people turned up including the Duke of Devonshire, but although the concert was an excellent advertisement for Hanbury's schemes, it barely met its costs.

Unfortunately by the time of Hanbury's death in 1778, the foundation had only made about one-fiftieth of the money required. Not surprisingly his major plans never materialised, although other smaller schemes have subsequently benefited from his charity. The fund also helped to build Church Langton's organ, the instrument used for the first ever performance of Handel's "Messiah" in an English parish church.

If Hanbury's plans for the Langtons seem extraordinary, so too was the Hanbury mausoleum which he had built in the south-east corner of Church Langton churchyard:

> "... the mausoleum ... the inside of which, by his own direction is of the best stucco, and a bright yellow. One coffin is covered with black velvet and ornamented with silver furniture; which are to be repaired as often as they become tarnished.
> On a compartment opposite the door is placed the bust of the founder, and under it these words: 'I will not suffer mine eyes to sleep, nor the temples of my head to take rest, until I have found out a place for the temple of the Lord.' On the other side, over the door, is written, 'Thou O Lord, hast heard my desires, and has given an heritage unto those who fear thy name.' These compartments are black and the letters gold.
> The inside of the mausoleum is to be kept perfectly clean; and the door set open every morning, excepting in hazy, misty, or rainy weather, in summer by five in the morning till seven in the evening; decreasing in proportion till the winter quarter, when from ten till three in the afternoon may be found sufficient airing. And a cell is to be built for a woman of irreproachable character, who is to be allowed 2s.6d. a week to keep it in proper order." (John Nichols)

At the time of St. Peter's restoration in 1865–6, the mausoleum was demolished and the coffins it housed were removed to a vault beneath the new vestry. The remains of the octagonal base of the mausoleum can still be seen in the churchyard, whilst inside the church above the door leading from the chancel to the vestry is a portrait bust of Hanbury.

Selina Hastings, Countess of Huntingdon (1707-1791)
Ashby-de-la-Zouch, St. Helen

foundress of the Countess of Huntingdon's Connexion

The Hastings were once one of the most prominent families in Leicestershire. Individuals of note or notoriety have included Lord William Hastings, Lady Flora Hastings and the "Mad Marquis" of Hastings. Their family chapel is to be found inside St. Helen's Church at Ashby-de-la-Zouch. Of those Hastings whose remains are interred there, the most outstanding personality was Selina, Countess of Huntingdon, a Shirley by birth, cousin of the notorious Laurence Shirley 4th Earl Ferrers (q.v.) and wife of the 9th Earl of Huntingdon (1696-1746). Lady Selina's memory is perpetuated at St. Helen's both by the fine commemorative brass set into the chancel floor and by the Annunciation window at the west end of the church. But more impressive is the outstanding portrait bust of her by Rysbrack, part of the fifteen feet high monument to her husband which stands at the south-eastern end of the Hastings Chapel. The inscription below was written by Lord Bolingbroke.

Regarded as the most celebrated woman in Ashby's history, it was claimed in Lady Selina's funeral sermon that she was the greatest woman in the cause of the Gospel of Jesus Christ that ever lived in the world. Pious in the extreme, she is best remembered today as the foundress of a sect of Methodists known as the Countess of Huntingdon's Connexion.

Her lifetime coincided with England's eighteenth century spiritual revival and the growth of evangelical preaching. Deeply impressed by the movement, she became a methodist early in life, and actively championed the nonconformist cause until her death. She opened her doors to many of the movement's preachers, providing them with a safe haven to stay and to preach. John Wesley frequently visited the family home at Donington and dedicated a collection of poems to her. Referred to locally as "Lady Bountiful", it has been estimated that she spent as much as £100,000 during her lifetime on religious purposes. She built chapels at Brighton, Bath, Tunbridge Wells, Worcester, and elsewhere, and in 1768 established her own theological college at Trevecca House near Talgarth in Wales. The college moved to Cheshunt, Hertfordshire in 1793 and to Cambridge in 1903.

Lady Selina died on 17th June 1791 and was interred in the family vault beneath the chancel of St. Helen's.

Top section of the 9th Earl of Huntingdon's monument, Ashby-de-la-Zouch St. Helen, showing Lady Selina Hastings mourning his death

Reverend Edward Stokes (1706-1798)
Blaby, All Saints

a remarkable clergyman

When the Reverend Edward Stokes erected the memorial to his family inside All Saints' at Blaby, he included his own name to "save trouble, and preserve the uniformity of the stone", avoiding any problems with dates by declaring that they were all interred there "in the eighteenth century". This almost proved incorrect in his own case though, for he lived to be ninety-two, dying in 1798. The memorial hangs on the east wall near the altar and is painted in gold and blue, attractively decorated with carved flowers.

Edward Stokes was one of the most remarkable members of Leicestershire's eighteenth century clergy. Despite having been left totally blind by a childhood accident, he took up an active career in the church and hunted regularly. For fifty years he was vicar of Blaby where he carried out his duties with little assistance apart from having someone to read the lessons. Few strangers encountering him for the first time realised that he was blind. He hunted briskly, being accompanied by a person who rang a bell when it was time to take a jump.

Enthusiastic about pastoral care and schooling, he used much of his private fortune for charitable works. He built a school at Countesthorpe (its site now occupied by the Church Rooms), and continued similar work begun by his father at Blaby. The local primary school on Queens Road at Blaby, although not the original building, still bears the Stokes name.

John Ellis (1789-1862)
Leicester, Welford Road Cemetery

England's third oldest railway line

John Ellis was one of the outstanding railway pioneers of the nineteenth century. A Quaker farmer turned industrialist, his early efforts were largely responsible for bringing the Leicester and Swannington Railway into being. It was the third railway line in the country, the first in Leicestershire, and later became the oldest part of the Midland Railway Company.

Initial credit for the scheme must however go to local mine owner William Stenson, who, having witnessed construction in progress on the Liverpool and Manchester railway, quickly saw the potential of such a line to link the north-west Leicestershire coalfields with consumers in Leicester. He surveyed a likely route and set out the details in a letter to Ellis. Impressed by Stenson's suggestion, Ellis directly approached George Stephenson for help. Stephenson was too busy to engineer the line himself, and arranged for his son Robert to do the job instead. Construction began at Leicester's West Bridge in October 1830, and by summer 1832 the first section to Bagworth was complete. On 17th July that year, the inaugural journey took place, carrying over 400 people, most of them in open coal waggons. The line was subsequently extended beyond Bagworth to Swannington. Passenger trains regularly ran on the line until 1928 and although the West Bridge to Desford section closed completely in 1966, part of the line from Desford westwards remains in use for goods trains. A small section of the second West Bridge station has recently been restored and incorporated in the Rally Park at the back of Tudor Road, Leicester.

John Ellis' monument in the south-west corner of Leicester's Welford Road Cemetery.

Later, Ellis played an important role in developing the rest of Leicestershire's early railway network. He was a pioneer and chairman of the Midland Railway Company, and helped establish the standard gauge rather than the broad gauge for railways in this country. He was also active in public life, serving as an Alderman, a Justice of the Peace, and a Member of Parliament. In 1847 he bought the Belgrave Hall estate where he lived with his family until his death. His daughters continued to live there until the 1920's. The Hall is now a museum.

His death occurred on Sunday 26th October 1862. The funeral took place the following Saturday. Ten mourning coaches and a carriage containing the servants followed the horse-drawn hearse as it left Belgrave. Many others including former employees, a number of private carriages, and several cabs joined the procession as it made its way to the Welford Road Cemetery. In places the streets were crowded with spectators, and shutters on some shops and many private houses were closed until after the funeral. His grave lies in the higher south-west corner of the cemetery where his small but attractive relief-carved stone, together with those commemorating his wife and daughter, stand out in sharp contrast to the grander monuments which surround them.

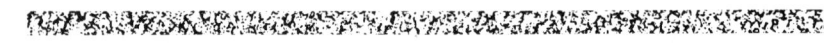

John Biggs (1801-1871)
Leicester, Welford Road Cemetery

an enlightened Leicester radical

One of the few people Leicester has honoured with a public statue is John Biggs whose figure in Welford Place is a landmark familiar to many. Yet had the original plans of the "principal men of the town" gone ahead, the memorial would have been confined to a more modest monument over his grave in Leicester's Welford Road Cemetery. However, the people of the town preferred the idea of a statue and readily contributed sufficient funds.

John Biggs' monument hides beneath the ivy, next to the obelisk commemorating his brother William, Welford Road Cemetery Leicester

Although at the time of his death John Biggs had been completely retired from the public eye for some ten years, the reputation he had established during the preceding decades still endured. He had been an outstanding Leicester figure both in business and in politics. As a businessman he had helped establish his family firm as one of Leicester's leading hosiery manufacturers and the largest employer in the town. He developed a reputation as an enlightened employer and was considered by many to be one of the best to work for. He was also actively involved in radical politics, becoming one of the first members of the new reformed Corporation in 1836. In 1840 he was elected Mayor, and twice again in 1847 and 1855. From 1855 to 1862 he represented Leicester as a Liberal M.P. As well as contributing to political reform and working class welfare, he pressed for many civic improvements including provision for Leicester's first municipal cemetery, choosing the land near the Welford Road for its site. He also had a reputation for charity and personal generosity. In 1861 however, the family firm collapsed and not long afterwards he withdrew from politics following a crisis in the Liberal party. He died on 4th June 1871 and was buried in the highest part of the Welford Road Cemetery. His statue was unveiled in Welford Place two years later. The present statue is a bronze replacement of the marble original.

Joseph Dare (1800-1883)
Leicester, Welford Road Cemetery

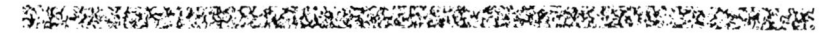

an early inner city social worker

"The faithful spirit... we commit to the grave to-day must be numbered amongst those who are the truest benefactors of the human race. His place amongst these was neither a very conspicuous nor a very influential one, but he belonged to the real saviours of men ... He lived, not for the honours or the rewards that have for the majority the greatest charm, but ... went about doing good... a teacher of the ignorant, a helper of the struggling, a guide to the doubtful, a consoler of the sorrowing. He was an educational and sanitary reformer before educational and sanitary reform became common property and popular. He advocated, more than a generation ago, a national and compulsory system of education .. . Working men and women trusted him and loved him. Many of these... he taught to think, to read with intelligence, or to take an interest in stirring questions."

(Funeral address for Joseph Dare)

Joseph Dare is one of Leicester's less well-known worthies. A pioneering social worker in pre-welfare state Victorian days, he worked for the Leicester Domestic Mission, selflessly devoting some thirty years of his life to help improve conditions for thousands of people in the town.

The private abodes of the Irish especially demand superintendence. It is a custom with them in taking a house, for one responsible person to rent it, but ten or a dozen others also make it their nightly rendezvous after their wanderings for rags and bones, and such things—or for the sale of wood in all directions. I went myself to one of these houses at the request of a benevolent gentleman, to see to the requirements of an Irishman who had been taken ill in one of his fields. I called on a Sunday morning, and then counted nine men, two women without shoes or stockings, and several children; all inmates of a place scarcely large enough for a single family. It is probable that more than these crept in here "under night's sable cloak," for Paddy Cardimugh was brought in from the street to answer my inquiries. The Scripture-reader whose especial business is to visit the Catholic Irish, informed me that as many as twenty grown-up persons may be often found herding together in these private houses. Filth, degradation, and disease are the sure results. I am happy to say that the new cottages now being built are of an improved construction.

The completion of the WATER WORKS will be a great blessing to the town. I have heard during the summer innumerable complaints of the failure of this indispensable element: quantity and quality are both at fault. I can speak feelingly here, for my own supply has failed every week for a long time. A person whom I regularly visit complains that fourteen houses in his locality are without a pump, and that he is obliged literally to steal his water when the possessors of private pumps are out of the way. Another intelligent friend, residing in quite a different part of the town, complains of water, "not fit to drink," for his own and a dozen other households. Add to this the present abominable state of the DRAINAGE throughout the town, and we cannot wonder, though we may not cease to grieve, at the alarming sickness and mortality that, of late, have afflicted more or less all classes of the inhabitants. From the far villas on the London-road, to the extremities of "the North" and Belgrave-gate, fever and diarrhœa have spread their desolating blight.

Extract from Joseph Dare's 7th annual report for the Leicester Domestic Mission 1852 (by permission of Leicestershire Libraries and Information Service)

Help was certainly needed. Living conditions in many parts of early Victorian Leicester were shocking. Closely packed shabby houses with neither proper ventilation nor sanitation; frequent infestations of vermin; large families often cramped into one or two rooms living without proper washing facilities or water supplies, in areas where misery, drunkenness, violence and vice were all too common. Dare spent much of his time in the northern part of the town known as All Saints Open, where conditions were particularly bad. On average he made some 4,000 home visits a year. His annual reports of the Mission's activities provide a fascinating insight into nineteenth century Leicester.

Dare died on Thursday 6th September 1883 at the age of eighty-three. His funeral the following Tuesday was conducted in accordance with his wishes "with the utmost simplicity that it might serve as a protest against useless expenditure and display". His gravestone in Leicester's Welford Road Cemetery, not far from that of William Gardiner (q.v.), is appropriately very simple and briefly alludes to his thirty years as minister to the poor of Leicester.

Edward Thring (1821-1887)
Uppingham, St. Peter and St. Paul

an influential educationalist at home and abroad

Edward Thring was a prominent educationalist who had a considerable influence on education both here and abroad. His writings were widely read in America, where a number of schools were founded based on his principles. He founded the Headmasters' Conference, established the first public school mission in London, and was a pioneer of further education for girls.

He was also responsible for transforming Robert Johnson's (q.v.) educational foundation at Uppingham into one of the foremost public schools in England. Appointed headmaster in 1853, he took it over as a small provincial school with twenty-five boys, two masters, a lack of accommodation, and with little reputation beyond the town. Thirty-four years later, at the end of his headship, it had over 300 boys, eleven boarding houses, thirty masters, and a growing national reputation. During this time, Thring had improved the school's facilities beyond all recognition and put into practice many innovative educational ideas.

Thring's seated statue can be found within the school buildings. Not far away, at the bottom of the steep path leading from the south porch of St. Peter and St. Paul, is a very tall handsome cross which marks the site of his grave. The monument was erected "by those of his boys who were at Uppingham".

Thomas Cook (1808-1892)
Leicester, Welford Road Cemetery

founder of Thos. Cook & Co., father of the modern travel industry and originator of the package tour

For some time up until the 1970's, an unsuspecting visitor to Leicester's Welford Road Cemetery could easily have walked past a certain ivy-covered grave without realising that it marked the last resting place of Thomas Cook, Leicester's most famous resident. Then in 1975, when the well-known travel firm which he founded got to hear about its condition, they not only renovated the monument, but also added the following tribute:

> "THOMAS COOK
> PIONEER OF TRAVEL · FOUNDER OF THE
> WORLD'S LARGEST · TRAVEL ORGANISATION
> FIRST · EXCURSION
> LEICESTER TO · LOUGHBOROUGH 1841
> ROUND THE · WORLD 1872
> HE BROUGHT TRAVEL · TO THE MILLIONS"

Cook's birthplace is just over the Leicestershire border at Melbourne in Derbyshire where as a young boy he worked first as a gardener's help and later as a trainee wood-turner. In 1828 he became a rural missionary for the Baptist Church covering some 2,000 miles on foot in 1829 alone. Several years later, when funds ran out, he returned to cabinet-making, setting up business first at Barrowden and then Market Harborough. As a committed teetotaller he also had a growing involvement with the temperance movement.

Thomas Cook's first passenger train excursion 1841 as portrayed on a frieze above a shop in Leicester's Gallowtree Gate

In 1841 he organised the famous first passenger train excursion from Leicester's Campbell Street Station to Loughborough. Its purpose was to take people to the temperance fête at Loughborough. He not only chartered the train and took responsibility for selling tickets, but also acted as conductor-cum-courier to the 570 passengers who had each paid one shilling for the return trip. Each passenger also received a small guide book to the route, written and printed by Cook himself. The excursion was a success and afterwards he was greatly in demand to arrange further outings.

In Autumn that year he moved to Leicester, setting up as a printer and publisher with his wife running a local temperance boarding house. As well as these activities the travel business was also expanding. Tickets for his first commercial "pleasure" trip to Liverpool in 1845 sold out quickly. The following year saw the start of a successful annual rail and steamer excursion to Scotland, whilst in 1851 as organiser of the Midland Railway Company's Great Exhibition operations, he took some 165,000 provincial visitors to the festival.

Further details from the Gallowtree Gate frieze showing transport to the Great Exhibition in 1851

By the mid-1850's the excursion business was becoming a full-time occupation. Operations expanded as the rail network developed. Excursions to the seaside became popular even if it did mean starting off at midnight! By the 1860's the first package tours to Switzerland, France and Italy were available for the better off. American operations started in 1865 and in 1872 the first around the world trip took place.

Much hard work went into organising the tours with Cook personally undertaking most of the negotiations with the railway companies, shipping lines and hotels. His family were often co-opted into helping, and when the business moved headquarters from Leicester to London in 1865, his son John Mason Cook became the extremely able manager of the London office whilst his father remained in Leicester.

Thomas Cook died in Leicester at "Thorncroft" (now the Leicestershire H.Q. of the British Red Cross Society, 244 London Road) on 18th July 1892. Thousands turned out on the bright summer afternoon for the funeral. Only ticket-holders were admitted to the small cemetery chapel (since demolished). Others waited by the graveside. It was a doubly sad day for the Leicester Temperance Society who saw both their President (Cook) and their Vice-president (Watkin Lewis Faire), buried on the same day.

Thomas Cook's balustraded monument, Welford Road Cemetery Leicester

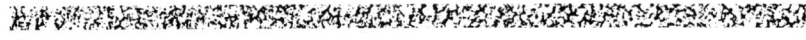

Charles Booth (1840-1916)
Thringstone, St. Andrew

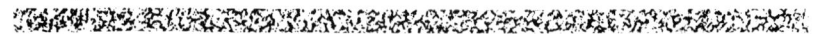

"the grimmest book of its generation"

Situated close to the path in the northern part of St. Andrew's churchyard at Thringstone is the gravestone of a nationally famous pioneer of social research. Made of white marble, rectangular in shape and lying flat upon the ground, it bears the name of Charles Booth, who as the inscription tells:

"DURING MANY YEARS, HE DEVOTED
THE LEISURE OF AN ARDUOUS LIFE
TO A STUDY OF THE CONDITION
OF THE POOR IN LONDON.
HE DILIGENTLY SOUGHT FOR
A FOUNDATION ON WHICH REMEDIES
COULD BE SECURELY BASED,
AND LIVED TO SEE THE
FULFILMENT OF A PART OF HIS HOPES,
IN THE LIGHTENING OF THE BURTHEN
OF OLD AGE AND POVERTY."

Booth was a Liverpool shipping line businessman who was actively interested in working class welfare. His outstanding achievement was a twenty year investigation into poverty in London, the results of which were published between 1889 and 1903 in his monumental work "Life and labour of the people in London". Called by "The Times" the grimmest book of its generation, it is an invaluable source for anyone with an interest in late nineteenth century London. The survey took many years of painstaking work. It involved not only Booth himself, but also a large team of investigators and helpers, including his wife Mary, the granddaughter of the great reformer Zachary Macaulay. Work began in 1886, the same year that the Booths moved to Grace Dieu Manor in Leicestershire, now the preparatory school for Ratcliffe College.

Amongst the pages of Booth's "Life and labour of the people in London", the conditions of individual families are recorded. For example, sharing one room at number 31 Tabernacle Yard were a very poor family of four supported by the wife. Her husband is described as being lazy, out of work a great deal, and although not a regular drunkard, spending his time at the public house. Elsewhere, a slightly better off family of five living in four rooms at number 16 Shakespear Place were country people from Leicestershire, the husband doing fairly well as a corn wharf labourer, and his wife working hard to keep house despite having bad legs.

Booth was also an active campaigner for the welfare of the elderly, his efforts contributing greatly towards the passing of the Old Age Pensions Act in 1908.

The Booths are still remembered with affection in Thringstone today. They supported various local projects including the foundation in 1911 of a social institute for the people of the village. Known as "Thringstone House", the building stands on the main street and is now the local community centre.

Booth died at his Leicestershire home in November 1916. The plain oak coffin was conveyed to St. Andrew's early in the afternoon of the 26th where with a guard from the Whitwick and Thringstone Volunteers, it rested on the chancel steps for several hours prior to the service. Outside in the churchyard, a magnificent collection of tributes formed a bank of flowers near the simple, ivy-lined earth grave. Further afield, a tablet was unveiled to his memory in the crypt of St. Paul's Cathedral, London in 1920.

Amos Booth (1843-1926)
Leicester, Welford Road Cemetery

champion of the anti-vaccination movement

As legislation during the latter part of the nineteenth century made it compulsory for all children to be vaccinated against smallpox, a vociferous national anti-vaccination movement grew up. Leicester became the stronghold of the cause. One of the movement's leading champions was local window-blind and packing case manufacturer Amos Booth, described at his death as the doughtiest fighter the anti-vaccinators ever had. Following the courage of his convictions he travelled the length and breadth of the country, zealously urging parents not to have their children vaccinated. Those who did eschew compulsory vaccination faced fines if prosecuted and found guilty, followed by the confiscation of property if unable to pay. As an expert on the vaccination laws, Booth defended many of the accused in court, often with marked success. He was himself prosecuted and imprisoned, but kept up his campaign until the right to opt out of vaccination on conscientious grounds was recognised in 1898.

Booth died at the age of eighty-two at his home on Knighton Lane in Leicester. His funeral service was held at the Belvoir Street Baptist Chapel (now part of the Adult Educational College), and afterwards his remains were interred in the Welford Road Cemetery.

Charles Bennion (1856-1929)
Thurnby, St. Luke

noted industrialist and philanthropist who gave Bradgate Park to the people of Leicester

Detail from the Bradgate Window at St. Luke's Thurnby, in memory of Charles Bennion

At the east end of the south aisle of St. Luke's Thurnby, is a colourful stained glass window depicting birds, flowers, a hedgehog, an owl, a rabbit and other creatures, as well as the prominent Leicester landmark "Old John". Known as the Bradgate Window it is a fitting tribute to Charles Bennion of Thurnby Grange, whose ashes are interred in Thurnby churchyard. Bennion, a prominent businessman and noted philanthropist, will long be remembered as the man who purchased the Leicestershire beauty spot Bradgate Park from Lady Jane Grey's descendants and gave it to the City and County of Leicester. Several plaques commemorating this gift can be found within the park.

Bennion came to Leicester in the early 1880's, as a partner in a firm which later merged with others to form the well-known and successful British United Shoe Machinery Company. For many years, he headed the company as its popular chairman and managing director. Like many contemporary businessmen, he also led an active public life, serving as a local magistrate, a "liberal" Conservative City Councillor, and President of both the Leicester Chamber of Commerce and the Engineering Employers' Association.

He died suddenly at the B.U.S.M.C. works on 21st March 1929 aged seventy-two. More than a thousand employees of the firm travelled by special train from Belgrave Road station to Thurnby to attend the funeral. Over 160 floral tributes were on display, many hanging on the columns and walls inside the church. A further memorial to him which stands over five feet high can be found in the north-eastern part of the churchyard.

Sir Mark Henig (1911-1979)
Leicester, Gilroes Cemetery

"tourist industry supremo"

When Sir Mark Henig died, many tributes were paid to the man who had "played a vital role in shaping modern Leicester and then went on to become one of the city's most distinguished ambassadors as a politician, businessman, and tourist industry supremo".

As "tourist industry supremo", Sir Mark energetically promoted the attractions of the English countryside, encouraging a new highly profitable industry. He joined the industry in 1969 as the first chairman of the newly established English Tourist Board. Initially on a three year contract, his success at the job kept him there for a decade. In a later interview he confessed to knowing little of what the job entailed at first, but could not resist the challenge of setting up a new organisation. His early tasks involved establishing the regional tourist boards and administering the Hotel Development Incentives Scheme. He also aimed at putting the less well-known areas of Britain, including Leicestershire, onto the tourist map.

Earlier in life Sir Mark gained prominence in local government, being one of the most dynamic figures in Leicestershire post-war politics. First elected as a city councillor in 1945, he served as a stalwart of the Labour group almost continuously up to 1970. He was twice President of the Leicester Labour Party. In 1958 he was made an Alderman; in 1965 High Bailiff; and was Lord Mayor of Leicester for 1967-68. The list of local and national councils, committees and organisations of which he was a member is lengthy and impressive. He also worked on consumer affairs, contributed greatly to the Jewish community and was actively involved in recreation in Leicester. His outstanding service to the community earned him a knighthood in 1965.

Although well travelled, Sir Mark took pride in his Leicester roots and lived for many years until his death at Stoneygate, Leicester.

Sir Mark Henig (by permission of Lady Henig)

6. Celebrities, heroes and sporting personalities

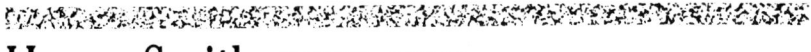

Henry Smith (1550?-1591)
Husbands Bosworth, All Saints

England's premier preacher

High up on an inner wall of All Saints' tower is a black marble tablet. Although difficult to see from ground level, the top part of the memorial portrays a family at prayer. Henry Smith, who is shown here as a young boy kneeling behind his father, was the most famous of this group. Born at Withcote Hall In Leicestershire, he grew up to become England's foremost preacher and one of the most eloquent lecturers in Europe. He made his name in London attracting crowds wherever he preached. His fluent and powerful speeches, together with his phenomenal memory earned him such titles as the "Miracle of his age" and "Silver-Tongued Smith".

Poor health cut his career short and in 1590 he retired to Husbands Bosworth, where he subsequently spent most of his time preparing his work for publication. He died before his highly regarded "Collected Sermons" was first published, and was buried at Husbands Bosworth on 4th July 1591.

Henry Smith's family ceased to be lords of the manor at Withcote after a later generation Henry Smith was committed to the Tower as a regicide for his part in the death of King Charles I.

Thomas Boothby (1681-1752)
Peckleton, St. Mary Magdalene

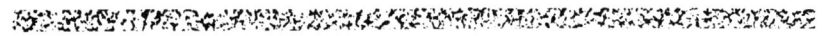

the first fox covert in England?

Set into the floor of the belfry at the west end of St. Mary Magdalene's Peckleton, is a large flat slab bearing the name Thomas Boothby of Tooley Park. Boothby was a famous early fox hunter and sportsman. His purpose-made fox covert at Tooley Spinneys was said to be the first in the country. He also claimed (but probably incorrectly) to have possessed the first pack of hounds in England. Tooley Park no longer exists but Tooley Spinneys can be found about half a mile south-east of Peckleton.

Reverend William Cave Humfrey
(1801-1874)
Laughton, St. Luke

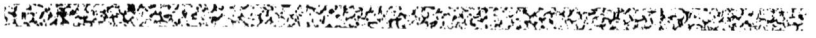

when hunting fixtures were read out in church

One of the best known sporting parsons was the Reverend Cave Humfrey, immortalized as Parson Dove in Melville Whyte's novel "Market Harborough". A familiar figure on the hunting field, he used to hunt at least four days a week. He was also one of the last clergymen to follow the practice in fox hunting centres of the parson reading out the weekly hunting fixtures in church.

As rector of both Laughton and Foxton, he lived at Laughton, and visited Foxton each Sunday to take the service. His performance in the pulpit was often highly emotional as he used to weep copiously during certain passages of his sermons. Once, an old lady, unable to attend church, asked to borrow the week's sermon. She was apparently much amused to read directions like "cry here" annotated in the margin!

Immaculate in appearance, he invariably wore a shiny black claw-hammer coat and low-cut embroidered waistcoat, usually set off by an outsize white cravat. Today he is remembered by a simple wall memorial hanging high up on the north wall inside St. Luke's at Laughton.

Reverend Edward Bullen (1795-1884)
Eastwell, St. Michael

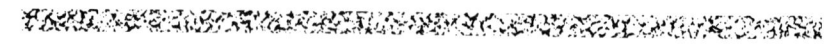

"Spurting Bullen"

St. Michael's at Eastwell is one of Leicestershire's architectural gems. It is also the church where the Reverend Edward Bullen was rector for fifty-four years during the last century. Bullen was a well known sporting parson who earned the nickname "Spurting Bullen" on account of his unfortunate habit of dashing his mount to the front of the hunting field.

Bullen began his sporting career after taking up a curate's post in Lincolnshire. However, his dashing tactics were strongly disapproved of by the local hunt, and efforts were made to have him moved. Lord Yarborough, master of the hunt, wrote to the Duke of Rutland saying that he had heard of a vacancy for a parson at Eastwell, and could thoroughly recommend Bullen as "a hard-riding lightweight curate who would doubtless make an excellent vicar". The so-called promotion to Eastwell was agreed and over the next half century Bullen enthusiastically pursued his interests becoming one of the best known faces on Leicestershire's hunting fields. Weighing barely eight stones, he rode horses that could carry no-one else, was easily recognised by his Tom Thumb size, and in true style would lead the field from the start, galloping off at full speed before his horse started to tire. He continued hunting into his late eighties, hated shirking, and enjoyed a hard ride across country even in his last few years. He always tried not to let hunting seriously interfere with his clerical duties, even if it meant turning up to take a funeral service in riding boots and spurs.

Bullen's memorial is in St. Michael's churchyard, not far from the chancel door. Its white marble cross has been broken, but the inscription is still there.

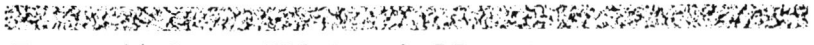

Bert (Albert Walter) Harris (1873-1897)
Leicester, Welford Road Cemetery

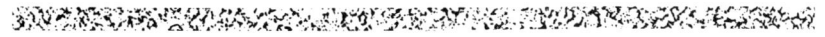

champion cyclist of England

Close to the cemetery railings at the Welford Road end of University Road, is a monument to world famous racing cyclist Bert Harris. The inscription on the flat stone scroll tells how the monument was placed there:

"BY THE CYCLISTS OF ENGLAND, AS A TOKEN OF THE SINCERE RESPECT AND ESTEEM IN WHICH HE WAS HELD BY WHEELMEN THE WORLD OVER. HE WAS EVER A FAIR AND HONOURABLE RIDER AND SPORTSMAN AND HIS LAMENTED DEATH CUT OFF IN HIS PRIME ONE OF THE BRIGHTEST AND MOST GENIAL SPIRITS OF CYCLEDOM."

Bert had a brief but phenomenally successful cycling career, and is without question one of Leicester's greatest sporting figures. His career spanned most of the 1890's and coincided with the great boom years of racing cycling when it became one of the main spectator sports.

Bert moved to Leicester from Birmingham at the age of eight. With encouragement from his father, he started cycle racing as a young teenager on the Aylestone Road track (now Leicestershire's County Cricket Ground). In 1891 he became a proud member of the London Polytechnic Cycling Club, England's greatest track club, and was soon chalking up numerous successes over distances from 400 yards to 25 miles. He rode not only in England, but also in Europe and Australia, overcoming strong opposition to win many awards and prizes. Initially an amateur, he later turned professional. He was Champion Amateur Track Cyclist of England and afterwards Champion Professional of England. Many regarded him as a future world champion.

At Easter 1895 he took a nasty spill at Cardiff, but recovered to ride his best season in 1896. The following Easter, with a sense of impending doom, he went off to race on the new cement track at Birmingham (now Villa Park). Following a puncture in an earlier race, he was about to withdraw from the main event of the day, when a last-minute offer of another front wheel saw him to the starting line. On the fifth mile he fell heavily hitting his head on the cement. The crash proved fatal and on 21st April 1897, at the age of twenty-three, he died in the Birmingham General Hospital.

Leicester turned out en masse to pay its last respects to Bert. On the day of the funeral the two miles between his house at Belgrave and the Welford Road Cemetery was so thronged with people, that according to the "Leicester Daily Post", such a scene had never before been seen in the town.

Cycling champion Bert Harris with his father (by permission of the Leicester Mercury)

Sir Henry St. John Halford (1828-1897)
Newton Harcourt, St. Luke
(Also commemorated at Wistow, St. Wistan)

"The Grand Old Man of Shooting"

Leicestershire County Council's first chairman was Sir Henry St. John Halford, a rifle expert of international repute and an all-round sportsman.

For over forty years he played a prominent part in local affairs, his services being officially recognised when he was made a Companion of the Bath in 1886. He served as County Magistrate; Chairman of Leicestershire Quarter Sessions; High Sheriff of Leicestershire; Deputy County Lieutenant, and chaired the County Council from 1889-1893. He was the much respected Honorary Colonel of the Leicestershire Rifle Volunteers, and amongst other offices, was also President of the local branch of the Cremation Society.

As a sportsman Sir Henry enjoyed shooting, hunting, fishing and sailing, and was as a young man, a member of the adventurous party which took the first English rowing boat on continental waters. Known in his later years as "the Grand Old Man of Shooting", he shot his way to many records, captaining numerous winning teams both at home and abroad. As a practical gun maker he had few equals, whilst his authoritative knowledge of small arms was often in demand by the British government. He had his own gun workshop at Wistow as well as a private range in a field near the Hall.

Sir Henry died at Wistow on 4th January 1897, leaving instructions that his body be cremated. With few such facilities then available, his remains were taken by train from Great Glen to Woking crematorium, being returned afterwards for interment at Newton Harcourt. His gravestone can be found in the south-east corner of the churchyard at Newton. Not far away amongst the Halford memorials inside St. Wistan's at Wistow is a rectangular wall plaque to his memory.

Reverend Robert Laycock Story (d.1898)
Lockington-cum-Hemington, St. Nicholas

cock-fighting in a church pew

The Reverend Robert Laycock Story has gone down in history for being the person who shot the last brace of grouse in Charnwood Forest and also on account of his passion for the unlawful sport of cock-fighting.

For almost a quarter of a century he was rector of St. Nicholas at Lockington-cum-Hemington. In his spare time he bred fighting cocks, regularly matching his birds against those of his close friend the Marquis of Hastings from nearby Donington Hall. One of their contests is reputed to have actually taken place in the church pews during a Sunday service!

Although there is no memorial at St. Nicholas' to the Reverend Story, the church houses a fine collection of monuments to his family and to their predecessors the Bainbrigges. The most outstanding of these monuments is the sumptuous wall memorial to William Bainbrigge (d. 1614) which fills a large part of the north wall of the chancel.

Tom Firr (1841-1902)
Quorn, St. Bartholomew

a favourite huntsman

Huntsman Tom Firr (by permission of the Leicester Mercury)

In a railed enclosure just outside the east window of St. Bartholomew's at Quorn, is a pink granite monument to Tom Firr "erected by some of his many friends and admirers".

Firr was one of the greatest huntsmen of all time. He was brought up in close contact with the hounds, his father having been a hound feeder with the Essex Hunt. Tom also entered into hunt service working as whipper-in to a number of hunts including the South Oxfordshire, Pytchley and North Warwickshire. Then at the age of thirty-one, he was offered the position of huntsman to Leicestershire's Quorn hunt, the most prestigious pack in England. He accepted and remained there at the pinnacle of his profession for twenty-seven years.

A superb professional horseman, he was greatly admired by those who followed his hounds. He was exceptionally skilful at organising the field and could be relied on to provide an exciting day's sport even on the most unpromising of days. He jumped fences fearlessly, never once losing his nerve. His career came to an abrupt end however, after a fall in 1899. Afterwards he received a testimonial of £3,000, the list of subscribers being headed by the Prince of Wales.

Firr died towards the end of 1902, and on a cold December day with a dull leaden sky overhead, a large solemn body of people gathered in the churchyard at Quorn to witness the interment of their favourite huntsman.

Reverend James Williams Adams
(1839-1903)
Ashwell, St. Mary

Thomas Ashford (1859-1913)
Whitwick Cemetery

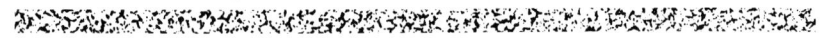

for valour

The Victoria Cross was founded in 1856 as Britain's highest award to armed service personnel for acts of conspicuous bravery in the presence of the enemy. Since then over 1,350 people have received the Cross, including almost 300 during the Crimean War and the Indian Mutiny, and over 600 during World War I. Considerably fewer awards have been made during the rest of this century, with the most recent during the Falklands War. The Maltese cross design for the medal was chosen by Queen Victoria, and the crosses are made of bronze from the melted down metal of Russian cannon captured at Sebastopol during the Crimean War.

Two outstanding early V.C. winners whose remains lie in Leicestershire are the Reverend James Adams and Private Thomas Ashford.

the first clergyman to win the V.C.

A tall cross on a stepped base in the south-west part of St. Mary's churchyard at Ashwell marks the grave of the Reverend James Adams, the first clergyman ever to be awarded the Victoria Cross.

Reputed to be the strongest man in Ireland during his youth, he was also a fine athlete, gymnast and horseman. He entered the church after graduating from Trinity College, Dublin, and for over twenty years worked amongst the army in India, winning his V.C. during the Afghan Wars on 11th December 1879 at Villa Kazi. With the enemy close by, he jumped into a ditch to save a group of men of the 9th Lancers who were trapped at the bottom beneath their horses. Waist high in water, Adams used his sheer strength to drag the exhausted men clear, before making his own escape on foot, whilst under heavy fire from the Afghans.

His recommendation for the V.C. was at first considered impossible, since the award was only made to servicemen and not padres. However, Queen Victoria intervened, the regulations were modified, and Her Majesty personally bestowed the award. Adams also won the bronze star, the Afghan war medal and the Burma medal.

Reverend James Williams Adams V.C. (by courtesy of the Director, National Army Museum, London)

Whilst in India, Adams worked amongst the many cholera and smallpox outbreaks, attributing his own escape from the diseases primarily to a glass of sherry drunk each time before entering camp. He also hunted, gathering his own pack to chase jackal. In 1886 he returned to England, becoming at first rector for Postwick in Norfolk and later for Stow Bardolph. Queen Victoria made him her honorary chaplain in 1900 and shortly afterwards he became a chaplain-in-ordinary to the new king. In 1902 however, ill-health forced him to take on the smaller living at Ashwell, and just over a year later he died there on 20th October 1903.

Amongst those present at the funeral were a representative of the King, and Lord Roberts.

There are also memorials to Adams at Peshawar Church in India and at Stow Bridge Church in Norfolk. This tiny church also houses the portable wooden altar and other items which he used during the Afghan War.

Leicestershire's first V.C.

The funeral of local postman Thomas Ashford was such an event, the like of which had never before been witnessed in Whitwick. On the day, the firing party paraded in front of his house in Skinners Lane, and in accordance with military practice, presented arms on the body as it was borne from the house to the ambulance carriage. An estimated 8,000 people from all over the country had come to pay their last respects, and in the streets leading from Skinners Lane to the cemetery, the crowds were so great that there was barely room for the cortège to pass. The procession made an imposing spectacle as it moved towards the Parish Church of St. John the Baptist where it was met by the Reverend Cheverton Shrewsbury, vicar of Thringstone. The Whitwick Holy Cross Band was assembled outside the churchyard gates and headed the procession to the cemetery playing the Dead March. Responses and a hymn were sung by the choir at the graveside. There were a number of magnificent wreaths including one from Charles and Mary Booth (q.v.) of Grace Dieu Manor.

Ashford was the first man in the old county of Leicestershire to be awarded the Victoria Cross, and England's only postman entitled to wear the award. He won it for bravery during the Afghan Wars whilst serving as a private with the Royal Fusiliers. On 16th August 1880, a party of British soldiers had come under siege from local tribesmen in the small Afghan village of Deh Khoja. Many of the soldiers were quickly killed. One however, a Private Massey, had managed to pull himself into the cover of a building. His desperate situation was noticed by Ashford and an officer named Lieutenant Chase, and together they formed a rescue party. The Regiment's Lieutenant-Colonel later recalled how he had seen Ashford and Chase emerge from the building carrying Massey between them. As they headed towards the main party about two hundred yards away, the Afghans started to fire heavily at them. Several times Ashford and Chase had to stop to get their breath back and at least once it was feared all three were dead. Finally amidst a shower of bullets and to cheers from the men, Massey was brought back to safety. Both Ashford and Chase were awarded the Victoria Cross for their courageous action, and were later presented with their awards in Madras in front of some 20,000 spectators.

Returning to England in 1884, Ashford settled at Whitwick, where he worked as a postman for over twenty years. Popular, kind and unassuming, he would rarely talk about his bravery and although he wore his V.C. on Sundays, it was usually concealed under a jacket. He died of bronchitis on 21st February 1913. His grave is presently unmarked, although the Whitwick branch of the Royal British Legion hope that one day a memorial will be erected on the site.

John Maunsell Richardson (1846-1912)
Edmondthorpe, St. Michael and All Angels

twice winner of the Grand National

John Maunsell Richardson was a famous amateur steeplechaser. He twice won the Grand National, riding Disturbance in 1873, and then on Reugny the following year. Nicknamed "The Cat", he was considered by many to be the best horseman and all-round sporting personality of his generation. At the time of his death, he was joint master of the Cottesmore Hunt. He lies buried in the southern part of St. Michael's churchyard at Edmondthorpe, his grave being surrounded by decorative metal railings. A commemorative tablet erected by his widow the Countess of Yarborough, can be found on the wall of the northern aisle inside the church.

Count William Elliott Zborowski (d.1903)
Count Luigi Zborowski (1895-1924)
Burton Lazars, St. James

"Chitty-Chitty-Bang-Bang"

Count Elliott Zborowski was a millionaire who made a name for himself both as a huntsman and as a racing driver. He was of Polish descent, his grandfather having been a Polish government minister who fled the country to America at the time of the Russian invasion. The Count later settled in England and became one of the many sporting aristocrats, who during the latter part of the nineteenth century, took up temporary residence in Melton Mowbray for the hunting season. Coventry House, where the Count and his family lived, still stands behind the Boat Inn in Burton Street.

Tall and very handsome, the Count was a fearless rider and a fine horseman. He was one of the leading figures in the Melton field for a number of years, and achieved the dubious distinction of second place in Lady Augusta Fane's infamous midnight steeplechase. Later he gave up hunting and successfully competed at motor racing but was killed in a motor racing accident at Nice in 1903. The Count's funeral took place back in England at Melton. The coffin was borne in an open car with a carriage containing the floral tributes at the front, and eight mourning carriages behind. Many local people were also present. The service was held at Melton and afterwards the Count's remains were taken on a bier to Burton Lazars, where they were interred in the family enclosure in the churchyard.

His son Luigi was likewise a famous racing driver and also a talented engineer. He helped build the car featured in the film "Chitty-Chitty-Bang-Bang" and was also responsible for constructing the first railway engine to be used on the world's smallest public railway at Romney in Kent. He too was killed whilst racing and was buried at Burton Lazars, his magnificent funeral leaving a lasting impression on the local people. The family grave lies enclosed by railings in the north-west corner of St. James' churchyard, not far from the extraordinary monument to William Squire (q.v.) The copper laurel wreath formerly on display by the grave was restored not long ago and moved inside the church.

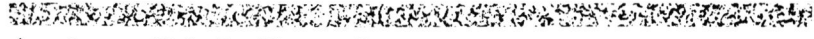

Arthur Dick Pougher (1865-1926)
Leicester, Welford Road Cemetery

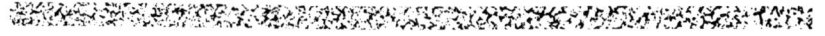

one of the finest all-round Leicestershire cricketers

Arthur Dick Pougher is widely acknowledged as one of the finest all-round cricketers that the county has ever produced, being best known for his outstanding bowling which is said to have "electrified" the cricket world. His most memorable feat was against the Australians at Lord's in June 1896, when for the M.C.C. he took five wickets in fifteen balls without a run, dismissing the visitors for a total of eighteen runs. The last six wickets fell with the score unchanged. In the same year he became the first member of the Leicestershire County team to complete one thousand runs in first class matches.

Pougher made his debut for Leicestershire at the Oval in May 1885, topping the bowling averages for that season. He played for the county until 1901, and from 1887 to 1909 was also a member of the M.C.C. ground staff at Lord's, during which time he took part in two overseas tours.

For many years he kept the Old Cricket Ground Hotel at Aylestone Park in Leicester, where he died in May 1926 at the age of 61. On the day of his funeral, the match in progress between Leicestershire and Northamptonshire was halted for two minutes silence as the procession passed by. He was buried at Welford Road Cemetery, but his grave is not marked today. Pougher Close in Sapcote, the village where he was born, was later named after the family.

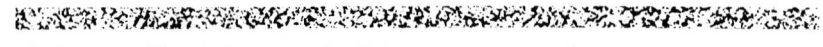

"Uncle" Edward Chapman Clayton (1837-1936)
Cottesmore, St. Nicholas

a large carved horseshoe in Cottesmore churchyard

Gravestones with illustrations and epitaphs especially appropriate to huntsmen can be found in various parts of the country. One of the best examples locally stands in the churchyard of St. Nicholas at Cottesmore. This particular stone marks the grave of "Uncle" Edward Chapman Clayton of Cottesmore Grange, a famous hunting figure in the Oakham area earlier this century. It features a large horseshoe carved in relief, inside of which is the following verse:

"WHEN YOU LAY ME TO SLUMBER
NO SPOT COULD CHOOSE
BUT WOULD SING TO THE RHYTHM
OF GALLOPING SHOES
AND UNDER THE DAISES NO
GRAVE BE SO DEEP
BUT THE HOOFS OF THE HORSES
WILL SOUND IN MY SLEEP."

A churchyard horseshoe, Cottesmore

Many of Cottesmore's gravestones have weathered badly, but this one is fortunately still readable.

Bennett Southwell (1913-1940)
Leicester, Gilroes Cemetery

for gallantry

The George Cross was instituted by King George VI in 1940 replacing the earlier Empire Gallantry Medal and the Albert and Edward Medals. It was intended as an award for outstanding civilian bravery but also came to be awarded to military personnel for acts of bravery in civilian situations. The list of George Cross winners is much shorter than that for the Victoria Cross, and today a George Cross award is a very rare event. George Cross medals are of silver, they are made by the Royal Mint, and are presented where possible at Royal Investitures.

One of the few George Cross winners with Leicestershire connections is Able Seaman Ben Southwell whose memorial is at Gilroes Cemetery in Leicester. Depicted on the stone is a carving of the George Cross.

Ben Southwell left his job at Corah's factory to join the Royal Navy at the outbreak of the Second World War. He trained at Portsmouth and later, unknown to his family, volunteered for bomb disposal duty.

On 17th October 1940 he had already successfully defused one unexploded bomb that day, when together with Sub-Lieutenant Jack Easton, he was called to deal with another in the East End of London. The bomb had crashed through a roof and had been left hanging through the ceiling, its nose six inches from the floor. The pair started work but barely a minute had passed when the device slipped. A chimney pot overhead collapsed and the bomb mechanism started to whirr into action, leaving the men twelve seconds to get away. Easton just managed to reach an air-raid shelter as the bomb exploded, but Southwell was killed as he tried to run to safety. The blast destroyed six streets completely.

In January 1941 Ben Southwell was posthumously awarded the George Cross for "great gallantry and dedication to duty".

Tommy (Henry Ernest) Atkins (1872-1955)
Leicester, Gilroes Cemetery

"doyen of British chess champions"

One of Leicester's greatest ever chess players was Tommy Atkins. Brought up on Fosse Road Central in Leicester and educated at Wyggeston School and Cambridge University, he took up a career in teaching. Keen on chess from an early age, he led the county team to victory whilst still a teenager. Later his name became well known in international chess circles and at one time admirers believed that he would be the next world champion. He played in many international matches and regularly participated in the annual cable match between England and America. His most outstanding achievement was winning the British championship nine times between 1905 and 1925.

The H.E. Atkins Memorial Chess Congress perpetuates his memory and has taken place annually since its inception in 1972.

Gertie Gitana (Gertrude Ross) (1887-1957)
Wigston Cemetery

famous music-hall star

One of the most eye-catching monuments in the newer part of Wigston Cemetery is a large white angel which stands next to the railings that separate the cemetery from the playing field. It marks the grave of music-hall variety star Gertie Gitana who made the song "Nellie Dean" famous. For over three decades she played to audiences up and down the country giving pleasure to many with her singing, dancing and saxophone playing. As well as "Nellie Dean", other sentimental songs which made her popular included "Silver Bell", "Never Mind" and "Kitty Dear".

Music-hall star Gertie Gitana

Gertie's connection with Leicestershire was through Wigston-born variety impresario Don Ross. Show business brought the two together at the Sheffield Hippodrome, and in 1928 they were married. She retired in 1937, but made a comeback shortly after the war to take part in the record breaking old-time music hall revival "Thanks for the Memory".

Reputed to be one of the richest women in variety, she supplemented her stage income by shrewd investments, often decided over a pot of tea and the "Financial Times" in bed in the morning. She once owned the Kilburn Empire before selling it to a cinema company.

Gertie came from the Potteries town of Hanley, where shortly before her death a road was renamed Gitana Street in her honour. She died in London on 5th January 1957. Her funeral service at London's Brompton Oratory was attended by many famous names. Afterwards her remains were brought back by train to Wigston and interred in Wigston Cemetery following a short service at St. Mary's Catholic Church. Over 200 people braved the cold wind to attend. Scores of wreaths from all over the country, many arranged as musical notes, hung over the railings at the edge of the grave as a last tribute to the person who for many was Nellie Dean. The striking monument was erected by her husband, and on its base, the inscription includes a verse from "Nellie Dean":

"THERE'S AN OLD MILL BY THE STREAM,
NELLIE DEAN,
WHERE WE USED TO SIT AND DREAM,
NELLIE DEAN,
AND THE WATERS AS THEY FLOW
SEEM TO MURMUR SWEET AND LOW
YOU'RE MY HEART'S DESIRE, I LOVE YOU,
NELLIE DEAN.

THE CURTAIN'S DOWN, THE SHOW IS DONE
AND WE ARE HOME AGAIN DEAR ONE."

Monument to Gertie Gitana, Wigston Cemetery

Don outlived Gertie by over twenty years. After the decline of the music hall, he ran a night club on the Costa Brava for a while and organised cabaret on the liner Queen Elizabeth II, as well as being agent for many well known theatre personalities. Known as "Mr Showbusiness", he succeeded David Nixon in 1977 as "King Rat" of the "Grand Order of Water Rats". Don died in February 1980. His funeral service held at St. Paul's Church Covent Garden attracted many celebrities. Afterwards his remains were interred alongside those of his wife in Wigston Cemetery.

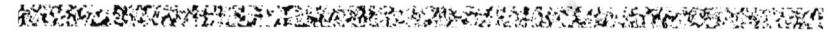

Wilfred Bollard (d.1977)
Slawston, All Saints

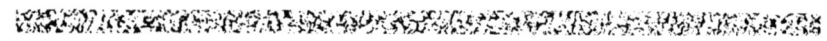

Leicester naval diver's world record

In 1948 Leicester-born Petty Officer Wilfred Bollard earned himself a place in the "Guinness Book of Records" by setting up a new world record for deep water diving. At the time he was one of a team of divers taking part in post-war Royal Navy experiments in Scotland to perfect a comfortable diving suit, which would be suitable for men working on rescuing trapped submarine crews. During this work, team member P.O. Soper of Essex became the first to break the eleven years old American diving record with a descent of 451 feet. Two days later on 26th August, after winning the draw to go down next, P.O. Bollard set yet another new record with a dive of 535 feet off Garvel Point, Tarbert. On reaching the bottom of the loch he spent some time walking on its muddy floor and later said he could have gone down a further 100 feet had the loch been deeper. His record stood until 1956.

Bollard left the Navy shortly afterwards but continued to dive commercially. In the 1950's he started his own business and latterly lived at Church Cottage, Slawston until his death in 1977. His memorial in the form of an open book stands in Slawston churchyard.

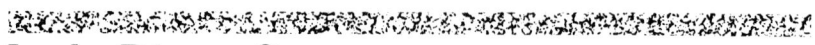

Lady Diana Cooper (1892-1986)
Belvoir Castle Mausoleum

"an exceptionally brilliant social figure"

Lady Diana Cooper was one of the greatest beauties of this century. For many years a leading light of high society, she possessed not only good looks but also intelligence, wit and tremendous charm. Her magnetic personality attracted countless admirers. In 1919 she married politician and diplomat Duff Cooper, who positions included Secretary of State for War, First Lord of the Admiralty, and British Ambassador in Paris. Amongst many other things, Lady Diana was for a while a successful actress and silent film star. She appeared in one of the first colour films to be made in Britain and afterwards created a sensation as the Madonna in Max Reinhardt's "The Miracle". Later, on abandoning the stage, she became increasingly involved in matters connected with her husband's career. Throughout her life, Lady Diana had a wide circle of friends and acquaintances, ranging from the respectable to the outrageous, of which her preference was said to be for the latter.

Lady Diana's individuality, eccentricities and hedonistic personality are best discovered through the words of those who knew her, and through her own memoirs. Many fascinating stories and amusing anecdotes have been attached to her name, not least about the notes she left on her car windscreen for the traffic wardens to read!

Lady Diana was the aunt of the present Duke of Rutland. As a child she had divided her time between the family home in London and Belvoir Castle in Leicestershire, and following her death at the age of ninety-three in June 1986, she was buried beside her husband at the family mausoleum which stands on a hilltop amidst the wooded grounds of Belvoir Castle.

Lady Diana Cooper and Duff Cooper 1st Viscount Norwich by Sir David Low c.1927 (by permission of the National Portrait Gallery, London)

7. Villains and victims

William Banbury (d.1676)
Lutterworth, St. Mary

"killed by robbers upon Over Heath"

Although villains are not generally commemorated by a monument or inscription themselves, details of their crimes may be found recorded on the tombstones of their victims.

A small slate of considerable antiquity standing near the main gate just inside St. Mary's churchyard at Lutterworth, tells briefly of a violent robbery which caused the death of William Banbury:

> *"IN MEMORY OF*
> *WILLIAM BANBURY*
> *KILLED BY ROBBERS*
> *UPON OVER HEATH*
> *NOV'R 25TH 1676."*

The spot near where the crime took place and where justice decided the robbers should meet their end, lies a few miles south-west of Lutterworth, at the junction of the Watling Street and the Lutterworth-Rugby road.

Richard Parsons (d.1683)
Braunstone, St. Peter

"an infernal stabb"

In some instances the supposed perpetrator of the crime was actually named on the victim's tombstone. One such example can be found quite close to Leicester in St. Peter's churchyard at Braunstone, where near to the Queen Anne porch, one of the oldest slabs in the churchyard reads:

*"HER LYETH YE BODY OF
RICHARD PARSONS
DECEASED YE 30TH OF MARCH 83
AGED 30
IS PARSONS DEAD?
YEA STAB'D BY WICKED LANE:
AND MUST LYE HERE
TILL ALL MEN RISE AGAINE.
BY LANE'S INFERNAL STABB,
YOUNG PARSONS DY'D
CAUSE IN A FRAY
HE WITH HIS FRIEND DID SIDE."*

The bottom line is now below ground level.

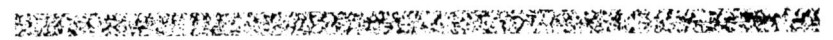

Richard Smith (d.1727)
Hinckley, St. Mary

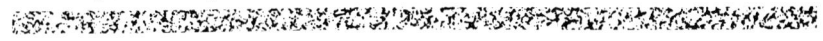

"justice took her flight"

Feelings of injustice caused by a murderer not being caught, coupled with threats of God's vengeance, can be found in Hinckley churchyard on a slab known locally as the "bleeding tombstone".

*"A FATAL HALBERT HIS MORTAL BODY SLEW:
THE MURDERING HAND GOD'S VENGEANCE WILL PURSUE
FROM SHADES TERRENE THOUGH JUSTICE TOOK HER FLIGHT
SHALL NOT THE JUDGE OF ALL THE EARTH DO RIGHT
EACH AGE AND SEX HIS INNOCENCE BEMOANS
AND WITH SAD SIGHS LAMENT HIS DYING GROANS."*

The victim was Richard Smith, a twenty year old saddler, who was murdered in Hinckley Market Place for making fun of a recruiting sergeant. The sergeant apparently lost his temper, charged through the crowd, halberd at the ready, and fatally wounded the young man in the chest. He then swiftly vanished, never to be caught.

Richard was buried in St. Mary's churchyard and for many years afterwards, mysterious blood-like stains were seen appearing on his tombstone each April as if to mark the anniversary of the murder. The stone originally stood under the east window of the chancel but was subsequently moved and now stands further back in the second row beyond the path. The bleeding phenomenon has since been explained as the effect of heavy rain washing out the colouring from a block of red sandstone above.

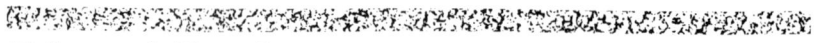

Edward Purdey (d.1743)
Old Dalby, St. John the Baptist

"she threatened to give me a mark"

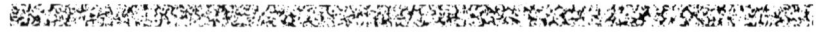

Friends and relatives of Edward Purdey wanted to make certain that a landlady's misdeeds would not be quickly forgotten and had the following inscribed on his tombstone:

"THROUGH A WOMAN I RECEIVED THE WOUND
WHICH QUICKLY BROUGHT MY BODY TO YE GROUND
IT'S SURE IN TIME THAT SHE WILL HAVE HER DUE
THE MURDERING HAND GOD'S VENGEANCE WILL PURSUE.
THE DEBT I OW'D THAT CAUSED ALL THE STRIFE
WAS VERY SMALL TO COST ME MY SWEET LIFE
SHE THREATENED TO GIVE ME A MARK
& MADE HER CAUSE LOOK VERY DARK."

The story is told how one evening in 1743, Edward Purdey had gone to drink at his local inn. When the time came to pay the bill, he was a halfpenny short. The landlady demanded payment in full, threatening to put a mark on him (bewitch him) if he did not settle. Finding her threats were to no avail, she is said to have let her dog savage him to death.

Purdey's revealing stone stands in the churchyard at Old Dalby, just inside the main gate near the left hand edge of the path.

Angel head decoration on Edward Purdey's headstone, Old Dalby St. John the Baptist

John Johnson (d.1760)
Breedon-on-the-Hill, St. Mary and St. Hardulph

Laurence Shirley, 4th Earl Ferrers (1720-1760)
Staunton Harold, Holy Trinity?

a silken cord for a hangman's rope

Standing high on top of Breedon Hill and dominating the surrounding countryside is the church of St. Mary and St. Hardulph. It is famous for its Saxon sculpture and for its monuments to the Shirley family who lived nearby at Staunton Harold Hall. In the south-eastern part of the churchyard is a reminder of a tragedy which caught the nation's interest, and led to one of the most sensational murder trials of the eighteenth century. Close to the path can be found a large upright stone commemorating John Johnson. Its inscription tells that he was for many years the "esteem'd and faithful servant" of the Hon. Laurence Shirley of Staunton Harold, and the incorruptible steward to his son the Hon. Laurence Earl Ferrers "till near the fatal period of his life" and his "untimely death". Not surprisingly there is no mention that it was Earl Ferrers who was responsible for Johnson's death.

Initially, the fiery-tempered Ferrers and Johnson had got on well together, and when Ferrers separated from his wife, he urged Johnson to accept the unenviable job of overseeing his wife's maintenance. Reluctantly Johnson accepted, but soon fell from favour when it became clear that he intended to administer the trust honestly. Ferrers decided Johnson would have to go, and tried to terminate his tenancy on the Staunton Harold Estate. When this failed, more drastic measures were resorted to. On 13th January 1760, having made sure that the hall was virtually empty, Ferrers invited Johnson over to his room. He locked both Johnson and himself inside. About an hour later Ferrers was overheard to say "Down on your knees, your time is come, you must die!". Shortly afterwards a shot rang out. A servant called to the scene witnessed Johnson covered in blood but still alive. The assistance of Dr Kirkland (q.v.) from Ashby-de-la-Zouch was summoned but there was little he could do and Johnson died early the next morning. Ferrers was arrested shortly afterwards and charged with murder. He was taken into custody first at a public house in Ashby, and then held at Leicester gaol before being transferred to London for trial by his peers at Westminster. A plea of not guilty on the grounds of occasional insanity was rejected and he was sentenced to hang at Tyburn. His request to be beheaded within the Tower instead was refused.

Lord Ferrers went to his death in style, travelling in his own landau and wearing his wedding suit of richly embroidered silver. The closely guarded procession took two and three-quarter hours to make its way through the crowds between the Tower and Tyburn. Ferrers was allowed the "privilege" of a silken cord instead of the common hangman's rope, and in meeting his fate he became not only the first man to die on the "new drop", but also the last peer of the realm to be hanged. Afterwards his body was taken to the Surgeon's Hall for dissection before being privately buried under the belfry of the Church of St. Pancras. According to tradition, his remains were later disinterred and brought back to Staunton Harold.

Laurence Shirley, 4th Earl Ferrers. His execution is portrayed below the portrait (by permission of the National Portrait Gallery, London)

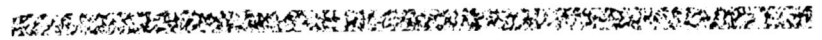

John Fenton (d.1778)
Leicester, St. Martin

"a sad example of the incompetency of juridicial institutions"

Gravestones are unexpected places to find criticism of the legal system, but not far from the south doorway of St. Martin's Church Leicester in a very prominent position, is an unusual stone with the following verse:

> "ENQUIRING MORTAL, WHO E'ER THOU ART,
> PONDER HERE ON AN INCIDENT, WHICH HIGHLY CONCERNS
> ALL THE PROGENY OF ADAM.
> NEAR THIS PLACE LIETH THE BODY OF JOHN FENTON,
> WHO FELL BY VIOLENCE, MAY 17, 1778
> AND,
> REMAINS A SAD EXAMPLE OF THE INCOMPETENCY
> OF JURIDICAL INSTITUTIONS TO PUNISH A MURDERER!
> HE LEFT TO MOURN HIS UNTIMELY FATE
> A MOTHER, A WIDOW AND TWO CHILDREN.
> THESE, BUT NOT THESE ALONE, ARE GREATLY INJURED,
> PERSONAL SECURITY RECEIVED A MORTAL WOUND
> WHEN VENGEANCE WAS AVERTED FROM HIS ASSASSIN
> BY THE SOPHISTICAL REFINERS OF NATIONAL JUSTICE.
> OBIT. ANNO AETATIS SUI 39".

Innkeeper John Fenton's untimely death was the result of a dispute which arose over a game of billiards between his brother James Fenton and a French officer named Soules. The game in question took place in Leicester at the Lion and Dolphin (formerly in the Market Place). Soules lost, and being unable to pay the six shilling wager immediately, was accused by James of defaulting. The following day when the two met there again, Soules, feeling his honour had been slighted, demanded either an apology from James, or to settle the matter like gentlemen. An apology was not forthcoming and Soules threw down two loaded pistols onto the billiard table for James to take his choice. James took one, but instead of fighting fled to show the weapon to the Mayor, for although duelling was not to be outlawed for another forty years, it was nevertheless regarded as a breach of the peace. With Soules in hot pursuit, James headed for shelter at his brother's inn, the Green Dragon. Soules arrived shortly afterwards, demanding the return of his pistol. Landlord John Fenton, a large stout man, who was doubtless used to dealing with troublemakers, tried to intercept the Frenchman and eject him from the premises but in the scuffle which followed, he was mortally wounded as the pistol discharged. Although Soules was quickly arrested and found guilty of manslaughter, he later received the King's pardon. Locally this was a highly unpopular decision as the curious epitaph on Fenton's gravestone suggests.

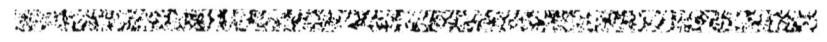

George Davenport (1758-1797)
Wigston Magna, All Saints

Wigston's Dick Turpin?

Names have been omitted from burial registers for various reasons. Sometimes the clerk or minister simply forgot to make the entry. On other occasions, details have been deliberately left out. In George Davenport's case it was most likely the latter, and all that the curious will find "written" about him in the 1797 All Saints' register is a dotted line. Perhaps not surprisingly, for Davenport was Leicestershire's most notorious highwayman. Born into an otherwise respectable Wigston family, he took to crime at an early age, and terrorised the district for almost twenty years operating mainly as a footpad. His favourite spots for hold-ups were the main roads south of Leicester. London Road provided plenty of scope as did the Oadby-Wigston Road, especially where the coaches slowed down to ford the Wash Brook which then flowed over rather than under the road. Enlistment provided a further source of income. Ever enthusiastic about the idea, he took the recruiting bounty on at least forty occasions, making sure to disappear quickly afterwards, often with the recruiting sergeant's horse as well as his money! Eventually he was sought by the authorities not only for numerous robberies but also for desertion from the army.

Davenport was extremely agile and athletic, as he once demonstrated by walking around the church battlements. He was also a master of disguise, and generally more than a match for most who sought him. Once, when caught for desertion, he was sentenced to 600 lashes but only received 300, the adjutant considering it pointless to continue the punishment as Davenport seemed oblivious to pain. As tales of his activities and boldness grew, locals and visitors alike came to fear his name. Parents even started to use the threat of "I'll give you to George" as a means of ensuring good behaviour from their children. Davenport's many victims included landlords, market traders, butchers and travellers, and although he acquired a reputation for being generous with handouts from his proceeds, he robbed the poor as well as the rich. Local feeling towards Davenport was mixed. Many dearly wanted to see him caught and made to pay accordingly. However, he could always count on having friends in the Wigston and Oadby areas who were willing to help when the law was in hot pursuit – partly out of loyalty to the old family but more likely because they received a good share of the pickings.

Davenport was captured and escaped on many occasions. By the time he was finally brought to justice in 1797, he had committed over 200 crimes. Increasingly reckless towards the end of his career, it was a relatively minor offence which caused his downfall. Caught poaching fish at Blaby, he was charged under an alias and remanded to gaol. On the way there he persuaded his keeper to stop for a quick beer at the Saracen's Head Inn. Unfortunately for Davenport, someone recognised him and pointed out his true identity. Subsequently put on trial for robbery, the court took just ten minutes to convict him and he was hanged at Red Hill, Birstall on Monday 28th August just after midday. The local press, perhaps not without some sympathy, commended his conduct on the day, describing him as "39 years of age, very personable, and extremely well made" possessing "more than a mediocrity of natural abilities". Afterwards his remains were permitted to be interred at All Saints. Wigston's answer to Dick Turpin, a local Robin Hood or a romanticised eighteenth-century mugger?

John Massey (d.1801)
Hung in chains on Congerstone Heath

"Topsy Turvey"

Gibbeting was the practice of hanging an executed criminal in irons or chains, usually in a prominent position near the site of the crime, in the hope that it would act as a deterrent to other would-be wrongdoers. As the body was often left hanging to rot for many years rather than being taken down for burial, it is now a matter for speculation as to the eventual fate of many an executed criminal's remains.

Gibbet post at the side of the road near Bilstone

Two reminders of gibbeting are preserved in Leicestershire. The first is one of the few remaining gibbet posts in the country. It stands about eight feet high surrounded by low wooden fencing and can be found near Twycross along the side of the road leading from Bilstone to the A444. A plaque fixed near the top reads:

"THIS GIBBET WAS ERECTED HERE A ¼ OF A MILE FROM THE SCENE OF A MURDER COMMITTED BY JOHN MASSEY FEBRUARY 1800".

Massey was an uneven-tempered, powerfully built man, who went by the name of "Topsy Turvey" on account of his wrestling abilities. In 1800, in a fit of anger, he kicked his wife into the mill stream at Bilstone. She died shortly afterwards and was buried at Congerstone. Massey was charged with murder and sent for trial at the County Assizes. Upon being found guilty, he was sentenced to death, along with five other prisoners whose offences included stealing cattle, sheep and property. All except Massey were reprieved before the judge left the town.

Massey went to the gallows at Red Hill, Birstall in March 1801. The local paper expressed concern about the distance of the site from Leicester, considering it "highly injurious to the interest of the labouring part of the community who gratify their curiosity at the expense of a day's labour". Afterwards Massey's remains were grimly hung from the gibbet on Congerstone Heath, where for a number of years, they were the destination of many macabre and instructional outings. According to tradition, Massey's skull was knocked down and carried off as a trophy. Later it was said to have been lined with silver and placed inside a punch bowl at an Atherstone Inn. By the end of the century, Massey's remains had disappeared completely and it is unlikely that his own wish to be buried between his two wives was ever met. Afterwards the gibbet post lay in a ditch, before being restored by Earl Howe of nearby Gopsall Park.

James Cook (1811-1832)
Originally buried Leicester at the junction of Saffron Lane and Aylestone Road. (Later Leicester, St. Leonard?)

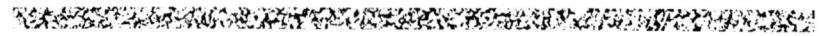

the gibbet's last victim

Leicester has the dubious distinction of being the place where the last gibbet in England was erected. The iron cage which once swung from its top is now in Leicester's Guildhall Museum. It was put up on Home Office instructions in 1832 to make an example of James Cook, whose appallingly gruesome crime has ensured him a place in history as one of Leicester's most notorious murderers.

Twenty-one year old Cook was a bookbinder in Wellington Street, heavily in debt, virtually penniless, and in imminent danger of bankruptcy. On the night of Wednesday 30th May 1832, one of his business contacts, a Mr Paas from London, called to collect an outstanding debt of twelve shillings. Paas was known to carry large sums of money with him.

In the gory events which followed Cook murdered Paas, took his money, hacked apart the body, and burnt the remains in his workshop furnace. However, he made the mistake of leaving the scene of the crime too soon. Flames from the unattended fire got out of control, and concerned neighbours, including the landlord of the Flying Horse Inn opposite, broke the workshop door down. Cook was fetched from his home in Wharf Street. His explanation that the horribly smelly object which could be seen cooking on his grate was mouldy horse flesh intended for the dog, did not satisfy those present and the local constable was called. Fortunately for Cook, Constable Measures had been on one of his regular tours of inspection to the local pubs, and according to reports, was in no fit state to handle the case. He put Cook on bail, deciding to leave a full investigation until later. Next day, the "horse flesh" was grimly identified as human remains. Meanwhile, Cook had broken bail and taken off northwards with the intention of fleeing the country. On reaching Liverpool, he went into hiding for several days, until a ship was ready to sail. It was as he was being rowed over to the America-bound "Carle of Carlton", that the law caught up with him. He was returned to Leicester for trial.

TRIAL OF JAMES COOK.
Wednesday, August 8.

Contemporary newspaper portrait of James Cook

Cook pleaded guilty, and within just a quarter of an hour, the death sentence had been passed. A vast crowd of over 30,000 attended the execution outside Leicester gaol. Afterwards, in accordance with Home Office instructions, Cook's body was taken and suspended in an iron cage from the thirty-three feet high gibbet post which had been erected at the junction of Saffron Lane and Aylestone Road. Further great crowds gathered to hold a "celebratory" fair beneath the ghastly towering spectacle. The scenes and reports so outraged opinion throughout the country, that the gibbet was taken down three days later, and Cook's body allowed to be buried there.

Almost a hundred years later, workmen digging a trench at the site were said to have unearthed the coffin, and in the 1930's there were rumours that Cook's body had been re-interred in the old graveyard at St. Leonard's Church, just beyond Leicester's North Bridge.

Samuel Adcock (d.1854)
Kirby Muxloe, St. Bartholomew

"fell by violence from the hand of an assassin"

In the case of unsolved murders, the guilty party was still sometimes referred to, as on a large upright slate in the western part of Kirby Muxloe churchyard:

"THIS STONE IS ERECTED IN AFFECTIONATE REMEMBRANCE OF
SAMUEL ADCOCK OF ASHBY SHRUBS IN THIS PARISH
ELDEST SON OF WILLIAM AND ESTHER ADCOCK, OF LUBBESTHORPE
WHO FELL BY VIOLENCE FROM THE HAND OF AN ASSASSIN,
AS HE WAS RETURNING HOME FROM LEICESTER ON THE NIGHT
OF THE 17TH OF JUNE 1854; IN THE 24TH YEAR OF HIS AGE
BOAST NOT THYSELF OF TOMORROW FOR THOU
KNOWEST NOT WHAT A DAY MAY BRING FORTH"

William Brown (d.1856)
Leicester, County Gaol (now Leicester Prison)

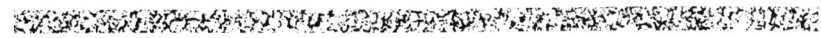

"Peppermint Billy"

In June 1856 a shocking double murder was committed near Melton at the Thorpe Arnold tollgate. Seventy year old gatekeeper Edward Woodcock was shot and stabbed to death, and his young grandson was found with his throat cut.

Several people came forward to help the police with their enquiries. One reported that a man had recently asked if the tollkeeper lived alone. Another told how the day before the murder, he had met a man cursing the old tollkeeper as a "snot-pot" for refusing him a drink of water. Matching descriptions of someone unable to stop blinking, coupled with several unusual finds at the scene of the crime, convinced the police that the culprit was Scalford-born William Brown. Nicknamed "Peppermint Billy" on account of his father's trade of making mints, Brown had a string of convictions for arson, theft and horse stealing. He had recently returned to England after serving thirteen years in a penal colony in Tasmania as punishment for a house burglary at Newtown Linford. The Leicestershire police launched an extensive manhunt on an unprecedented scale notifying Billy's description to forces throughout the country. Within four days, he was recognised at an inn at Wetherby in Yorkshire, arrested, and brought back to Melton by train.

A few weeks later, he was on trial for his life at a crowded Leicester Assizes where a verdict of guilty was reached. Attempts by the Society of Friends to obtain a reprieve were unsuccessful, and on 25th July an estimated 25,000 spectators turned out to watch Leicester's last public execution. Afterwards Billy's body was interred inside the gaol.

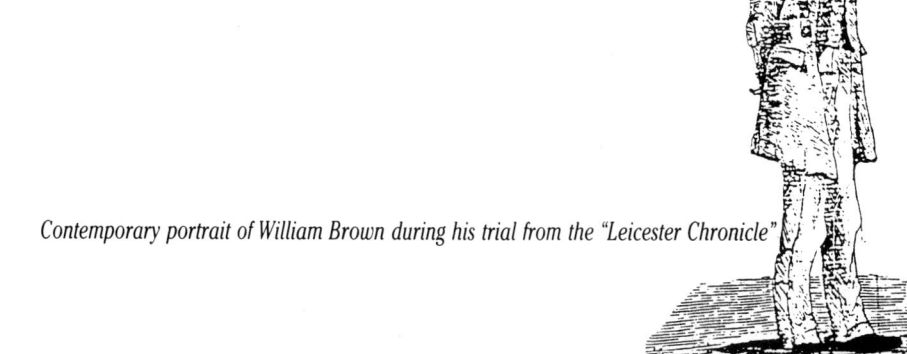

Contemporary portrait of William Brown during his trial from the "Leicester Chronicle"

Annie Bella Wright (d.1919)
Stoughton, St. Mary

the Green Bicycle mystery

One of Leicester's most celebrated murder trials was the Green Bicycle case earlier this century.

The victim was Annie Bella Wright, a good-looking twenty-one year old who lived with her parents in the village of Stoughton not far from Leicester. Late one summer's evening on Saturday 5th July 1919, a local farmer found Bella lying lifeless by the side of the road near Little Stretton, her bicycle close by and blood on her head. It looked like accidental death at first, but it was soon revealed as murder when a closer examination showed that she had been shot. Enquiries established that she was last seen alive setting off to cycle back from Gaulby to Stoughton, accompanied by a stranger on a green bicycle. Extensive enquiries were made, and Scotland Yard was called in, but no real progress was made at the time.

Bella Wright (by permission of the Leicester Mercury)

As the months passed with little of significance being discovered, interest in the case declined, until one day in February the following year, the frame of a green bicycle was found in the canal at Leicester. It was traced to Roland Vivian Light, a mathematics teacher in Cheltenham, who had been living in Leicester at the time of Bella's death.

Light was arrested and charged with the murder. His trial at Leicester Castle early in June 1920 kept the country on tenterhooks, as each day's proceedings were avidly reported in the newspapers. Sir Marshall Hall, one of the outstanding figures in English legal history, conducted Light's defence and with a superb performance managed to undo the prosecution's apparently watertight case. Light was acquitted and afterwards went to live in obscurity in Kent. No one else has subsequently been charged with Bella's death, and the case remains as Leicester's most famous unsolved mystery.

Bella's funeral at Stoughton drew over 9,000 people. Afterwards her grave lay unmarked for many years. In 1982 Alec Mackintosh of Evington published a booklet on the case, the proceeds of which went towards a memorial for Bella. Consequently, visitors to Stoughton churchyard today will find Bella's grave marked by a stone which reads:

> "IN MEMORY OF ANNIE BELLA WRIGHT
> DIED JULY 5TH 1919
> AGED 21".

The cruck-framed cottage where Bella lived is just round the corner from the church near the entrance to Stoughton Lane.

8. Accidents and misfortunes

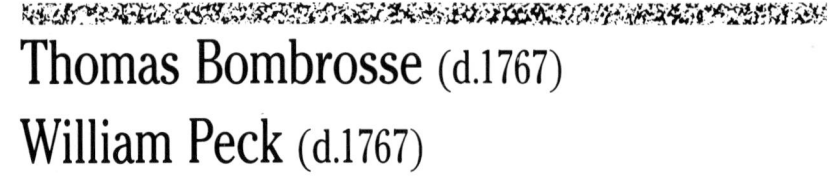

Thomas Bombrosse (d.1767)
William Peck (d.1767)
William Smith (d.1767)
Loughborough, All Saints

"a perpetual warning to all others"

Many accidents left their mark on the community, and it is not uncommon to find such events recorded on gravestones of the eighteenth and nineteenth centuries.

As well as commemorating the deceased, some inscriptions connected with accidents were also intended to serve as a warning so that others might avoid a similar fate. A slate erected in Loughborough All Saints' churchyard by voluntary subscription still warns:

> "HERE LIE
> IN THE SAME GRAVE
> THE BODIES OF
> THOMAS BOMBROSSE AGED 46
> WILLIAM PECK AGED 20
> WILLIAM SMITH AGED 18
> ALL OF THIS PARISH
> WHO WERE UNFORTUNATELY DROWNED TOGETHER
> IN THE RIVER SOAR ON THE NINTH DAY OF JULY 1767.
> IT IS PRESUMED THAT BOMBROSSE LOST HIS LIFE BY
> ENDEAVOURING TO SAVE HIS TWO COMPANIONS FOR HE
> ONLY WAS FOUND IN HIS CLOTHES.
> SOME OF THE PRINCIPAL INHABITANTS OF THIS PARISH,
> TENDERLY CONCERNED FOR THE SUDDEN FATE OF THEIR
> FELLOW CHRISTIANS AND FOR A PERPETUAL WARNING TO
> ALL OTHERS CAUSED THIS STONE TO BE ERECTED BY
> VOLUNTARY SUBSCRIPTION."

This advice is to be found amongst the stones set into the low grassy bank on the north side of the church.

Salutory gravestone, All Saints' churchyard Loughborough

Other similar local inscriptions reveal that death by drowning appears to have been a relatively common hazard even in inland counties such as Leicestershire. Watery accidents are also recorded in several churchyards at Burton Overy, Dunton Bassett and Long Clawson, whilst in the south-eastern corner of the churchyard at Barrow-upon-Soar, a stone to Joseph Taylor and Henry Barsby (d.1824) carries the following message:

> "STOP PASSENGER REFLECT UPON OUR FATE
> REPENT, BELIEVE BEFORE IT BE TOO LATE,
> TWO FELLOW-WORKMEN IN THIS GRAVE DO LIE
> BOTH IN A WELL AT BARLEY HILL DID DIE;
> TH' UNWHOLESOME DAMP THE FATAL STROKE DID GIVE
> AND WE AT ONCE ON EARTH DID CEASE TO LIVE
> GO MORTAL, AND LAMENT OUR EARLY FALL
> AND FEAR LEST DEATH THE NEXT ON THEE MAY CALL."

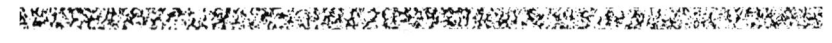

William Weston (d.1782)
Shearsby, St. Mary Magdalene

"catch'd in the wind mill"

In the southern part of the county is a reminder of the time when the countryside was dotted with windmills. A headstone in Shearsby churchyard just to the right of the main path bears witness to a tragedy of 1782:

> *"TO THE MEMORY OF WILLIAM WESTON*
> *WHO UNFORTUNATELY WAS CATCH'D IN THE WIND MILL*
> *AND EXPIRED THE 8TH OF SEPTEMBER 1782 IN THE*
> *16TH YEAR OF HIS AGE."*

Record of a windmill accident in Shearsby churchyard

Samuel Granger (d.1787)
Slawston, All Saints

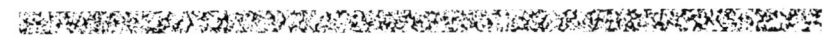

"a sudden change!"

Scattered throughout the county are a number of monuments which recall contemporary hazards. Especially notable are those which bear witness to the perils of road, canal and railway transport.

Samuel Granger was a waggoner and a native of Slawston who used to regularly carry goods between the Midlands and East Anglia. His activities came to an end one summer's day in 1787, when he was run over by his own waggon at Brickwall near Welwyn in Hertfordshire. His body was placed on top of a pile of goods on the waggon and brought back to Slawston for burial. The accident was briefly alluded to on his gravestone:

*"A SUDDEN CHANGE, I IN A MOMENT FELL
AND HAD NOT TIME TO BID MY FRIENDS FAREWEL;
THER'S NOTHING STRANGE, DEATH HAPPENS UNTO ALL,
MY LOT'S TODAY; TOMORROW YOU MAY FALL."*

Curiously when a second Samuel Granger died at Slawston some one hundred years later, the inscription was repeated on his stone. Two further, almost identical mid-nineteenth century repetitions of this verse can be seen in Gaddesby churchyard.

Thomas Hill (d.1796)
Willoughby Waterleys, St. Mary

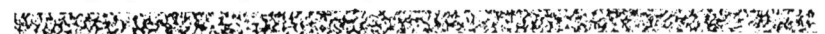

"killed in a tunnil near Saddington"

All over the country numerous lives were lost during the construction of the canals and railways, and many churchyards near the sites often bear humble memorials to the navvies killed in the all-too-frequent accidents. Sixteen year old Thomas Hill was one such victim whose gravestone in Willoughby Waterleys churchyard tells how he was "UNFORTUNATELY KILLED IN A TUNNIL NEAR SADDINGTON" on 17th July 1796. The tunnel was on the Leicester to Foxton section of the Union Canal and was part of a grand plan to link up the River Trent and the Derby/Nottingham coalfields with the Thames and London.

Thomas Wean (d.1807)
Shepshed, St. Botolph

"upon the road I met pale death"

Another carrier who met his death on the road was seventy-six year old Thomas Wean whose gravestone at Shepshed advises:

*"UPON THE ROAD I MET PALE DEATH,
WHICH SOON DEPRIV'D ME OF MY BREATH;
AND IN A MOMENT, AWFUL THOUGHT
MY SOUL ETERNAL MANSIONS SOUGHT,
FROM ACCIDENT, NO MAN IS FREE
THE NEXT OH READER, MAY BE THEE
THEN WHEN YOU VIEW MY GRAVE, MY DUST
PREPARE BE READY, DIE YOU MUST."*

Nathaniel Clark (d.1813)
Bisbrooke, St. John the Baptist

a waggon and horses carved in stone

A waggon and horses decorate Nathaniel Clarke's gravestone in Bisbrooke churchyard

One of the most unusual reminders of a road accident is a large illustrated upright gravestone which stands more than five feet high in the southern part of the churchyard of St. John the Baptist, Bisbrooke. It commemorates Nathaniel Clark, a local farmer who was killed when thrown out of his cart whilst travelling back from Empingham.

Carved in splendid relief across the top of the monument is a frieze of a four wheeled waggon being led by four horses. In the background is a barred gate, a fence and a building. Although much of the inscription is barely legible, the frieze is fortunately still quite clear.

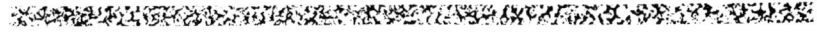

Michael Ingo (d.1834)
Kibworth, St. Wilfrid

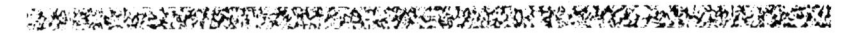

"killed by the upsetting of the express coach"

In 1834 a London express coach came to grief at Kibworth, killing an elderly gentleman from Nottingham. He was buried in St. Wilfrid's churchyard where there is a slate recording the incident along the north wall:

> *"IN MEMORY OF*
> *MR MICHAEL INGO*
> *LATE OF NOTTINGHAM:*
> *AGED 73 YEARS.*
> *WHO WAS KILLED BY THE*
> *UPSETTING OF THE EXPRESS COACH*
> *PASSING THROUGH THE VILLAGE*
> *TO LONDON,*
> *ABOUT MIDNIGHT APRIL 21ST*
> *1834."*

Not far away on the opposite side of the churchyard is a smaller stone to Roger Deacon who became a victim of the road at the age of twelve in 1780 when "DEATH PATROL'D THE NORTHERN ROAD."

Temple Crozier (d.1896)
Coston, St. Andrew

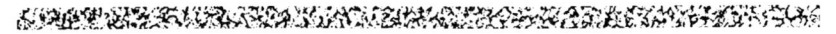

"stabbed on the stage"

Details of one of the most unusual occupational accidents to be recalled on a church memorial are to be found at the small Church of St. Andrew at Coston. Inside, on a large brass wall plaque near the altar, visitors are able to read how twenty-four year old Temple Crozier:

> "... WAS ACCIDENTALLY STABBED ON THE STAGE
> OF THE NOVELTY THEATRE WHILST PLAYING.
> THIS TABLET WAS SUBSCRIBED FOR BY SOME
> MEMBERS OF THE PROFESSION AS A SMALL
> TOKEN OF THE HIGH ESTEEM IN WHICH
> HE WAS HELD.
> A FAITHFUL FRIEND AND THOROUGH WORKER WHO
> DIED AT HIS POST AUG 10TH 1896. R.I.P.
> HE WILL LIVE IN OUR MEMORIES FOR EVER."

Crozier was in London at the time taking the part of the Spanish villian in a play called 'Sins of the Night'. Right at the end of the last act a stage knife failed to work properly and he was fatally stabbed in the chest. He dropped to the ground as the final curtain came down, the audience being unaware of what had happened as they left. A doctor was sent for, but on arriving found the victim of the accident to be dead. Still wearing stage clothes and make-up, Crozier's body was taken to St. Giles' mortuary the following morning, creating a scene which according to newspaper accounts, made "even the accustomed mortuary attendants pass more than their usual comment". Charges of manslaughter were brought against a fellow actor, but these were later dropped.

Crozier was buried at Coston on August 16th 1896 just outside the church porch. His family were well-known in the Melton area, his father a former army chaplain, being rector at Coston from 1889 to 1902.

A London theatre tragedy is recalled on Temple Crozier's memorial at St. Andrew's Coston

Ted (Edwin) Meadows (1843-1898)
William (Jack) Joyce (1869-1898)
Leicester, Welford Road Cemetery

"Faithful unto death"

A disastrous railway accident at Wellingborough is mentioned on two adjacent polished black memorials to Midland Railway colleagues at Leicester's Welford Road Cemetery. The accident happened on the 2nd September 1898. Ted Meadows was driving the 6.30 evening express from St. Pancras to Manchester. Jack Joyce was his fireman. Just as the train was due to pass non-stop through Wellingborough, a large heavy luggage trolley accidentally fell onto the tracks. An attempt to quickly move it out of the path of the oncoming express failed, and despite brave efforts by the footplatemen to slacken the engine's speed, disaster could not be averted. The train hit the trolley and ploughed into an embankment. Six people were killed and many were injured in the wrecked carriages. Amongst those who lost their lives were Ted and Jack. Leicester's Mayor paid a fitting tribute to their faithful service and bravery at the funeral.

Twin memorials erected by railway workers to colleagues, Welford Road Cemetery Leicester

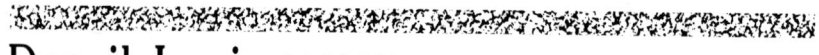

Denzil Jarvis (d.1912)
Commemorated at Knighton, St. Mary Magdalene

lost with the "Titanic"

A permanent reminder of the world's most widely known sea disaster can be found in St. Mary's churchyard at Knighton. Near the path leading to the lychgate is a tall stone cross. It commemorates Mr Denzil J. Jarvis, a former managing partner of Wadkin's Engineering Company, who was one of the four Leicester people who lost their lives when the "Titanic" went down on 14th April 1912.

Sea tragedies recalled elsewhere in Leicestershire churchyards include mention at Woodhouse of the sinking of the "King George" Packet in 1806 when William Beston lost his life "after near forty voyages to Ireland".

9. Sovereigns, courtiers and politicians

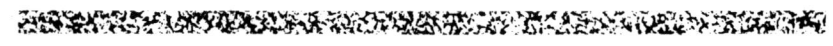

King Lear or Leir (9th Century B.C.?)
Leicester?

in a vault beneath the Soar

Not far from the spot where King Richard III's remains are believed to have been thrown into the River Soar, there is according to legend, an underground vault which was the burial place of King Lear.

Lear is believed to have been an ancient British king, who ruled for over sixty years some time around the ninth century B.C. According to Geoffrey of Monmouth, Lear was also the founder of Leicester and when he died was buried by his daughter Cordelia:

"... *in a certain vault, which she ordered to be made for him under the river Sore, in Leicester, and which has been built originally under the ground to the honour of the god Janus. And here all the workmen of the city, upon the anniversary solemnity of that festival, used to begin their yearly labours.*"

Cordelia, afterwards Queen of England as well as France, is also said to have been buried there, as was Archigallo, another British king.

Both the Jewry Wall and Holy Bones may have connections with the legendary vault, and several supposed entrances to its passageways were still being pointed out to visitors during the eighteenth century. The site has never been properly identified however, nor the legend substantiated.

King Lud (9th Century A.D.?)
Saltby?

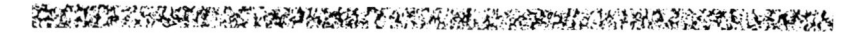

an ancient British ruler

Ordnance Survey maps covering the Saltby area in the Vale of Belvoir, show a feature known intriguingly as "King Lud's Entrenchments". The site lies west of a minor road running between Wyville and Saltby, where amidst the woods and remains of old building foundations, the more determined should find a linear bank and ditch earthwork about a quarter of a mile long. At the eastern end near Wyville Lodge are two barrows or burial mounds, one of which is called "The Tent". According to tradition this was the burial place of an ancient British ruler called King

Lud. Mystery surrounds the King's identity, although some believe he was Ludeca, King of Mercia, who was killed in battle in A.D. 827.

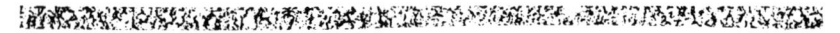

King John (1167?-1216)
Croxton Kerrial, Croxton Abbey
(and Worcester Cathedral)

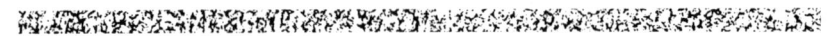

a notorious ruler's connection with Croxton Abbey

Leicester was the place where the barons first openly met to air their discontent at King John's rule, the outcome of this protest eventually leading to the signing of the Magna Carta in 1215. Further north in the county, within the walls of Croxton Park where Croxton Abbey used to stand, is the site of a twelfth century chapel which later housed part of the King's remains.

King John was one of England's most notorious rulers. He greedily extorted money from his subjects and squandered it in a selfish manner. He is reputed to have been abominably cruel, violent-tempered and vindictive, as well as being superstitious, irreligious, self-indulgent and scandalously immoral. Few historians have felt that his reign was anything other than a disaster. Much of his time was occupied fighting the barons, and after Magna Carta, he travelled the country trying to reassert his authority. A trail of devastation and destruction was usually left in his wake.

By early October 1216, the royal party was on its way from Norfolk to Lincolnshire. Whilst travelling across the Wash, disaster struck when the incoming tide caught them unawares, causing the loss of several lives as well as the Crown Jewels. The King himself narrowly escaped drowning and in a very wet and distraught state made for Swineshead Abbey, where, putting the traumatic events of the day aside, he got thoroughly drunk on the Abbot's wine and cider. The result was more than a bad hangover, and shortly afterwards, he lapsed into a fevered state. Barely fit to travel, he left Swineshead and continued with great difficulty to Newark, not far from Leicestershire's northern border. Three days later, despite receiving medical attention from the Abbot of Croxton Abbey, King John died at Newark Castle.

The Abbot of Croxton was probably aware that suspicion of poisoning might fall upon his brothers at Swineshead. Consequently whilst embalming the dead King, he took the precaution of removing any likely evidence including the King's bowels. These according to tradition were taken back to Croxton Abbey and interred in a stone chest in the chapel. As far as is known, they have stayed there ever since. Meanwhile the King's body was taken to Worcester Cathedral where it was buried in front of the high altar, between the shrines of St. Wulfstan and St. Oswald.

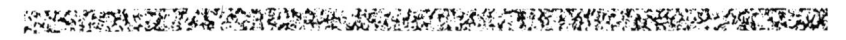

Robert de Roos (d.1285)
Bottesford, St. Mary
(also Belvoir Priory and Kirkham Abbey, North Yorkshire)

a heart burial

One of the most famous heart burials in England is author Thomas Hardy whose ashes are interred in Poets Corner at Westminster Abbey, but whose heart is buried in the churchyard at Stinsford, Dorset. In Leicestershire, a much earlier instance of this practice can be found in the northern part of the county at St. Mary's Church, Bottesford. There amongst the large stately monuments to the Earls of Rutland, is a small delicately carved miniature effigy of a knight, barely twenty inches tall. The figure is thought to represent Robert de Roos, one of the medieval Lords of Belvoir. When he died in 1285, his body was buried at Kirkham, his bowels before the high altar at Belvoir Priory, and his heart beneath the miniature figure at Croxton Abbey. Later, after the Dissolution of the Monasteries, both the effigy and the so-called heart stone were removed to Bottesford, where they are now on display in the chancel of the church that he founded.

Medieval heart burials marked by similar miniature effigies can be found in several other English churches. The example at Bottesford is slightly unusual in that the figure is not portrayed in the customary manner of holding a heart in the hands.

Miniature effigy, Bottesford St. Mary

Earls of Leicester (fourteenth century)
Mary de Bohun (d.1393)
Leicester, The Newarke

wife of a future king . . . princes of the blood

Mary de Bohun, wife of the eventual King Henry IV, lies buried in the Newarke, as do Henry Plantagenet Earl of Lancaster, and his son Henry Duke of Lancaster. The two Henrys were both princes of the blood, and also Earls of Leicester. They did much to establish Leicester as a leading medieval town, giving it a brief period of splendour hitherto unknown. Henry Plantagenet, described as a man of high character and sound judgement, was guardian to the young King Edward III. He spent his retirement in Leicester living at the Castle. Close by he built Trinity Hospital, and when he died in 1345 he was buried in the tiny chapel there. Not long afterwards his remains were moved to the new Collegiate Church.

His son Henry was known as the "Good Duke" and was the most outstanding of the Earls of Leicester. A successful soldier, statesman and diplomat, he was also a generous benefactor. The Collegiate Church in the Newarke was his finest gift to Leicester, and was reputedly founded to house a thorn from the Crown of Thorns, given to him by King John II in Paris in 1351. The Duke died during an epidemic of the Black Death at Leicester in 1361 having given instructions in his will just two weeks earlier that his body was to be buried in the new church. Trinity Hospital has survived, but there is little left of the church save a few fragments in the basement of Leicester Polytechnic's Hawthorn building.

King Richard III (1452-1485)
Leicester
(Also commemorated at Sutton Cheney, St. James)

last of the Plantagenets

Leicester is one of only a small number of provincial places that has the honour of being the last resting place of an English King.

Richard III, last of the Plantagenets, was buried in Leicester in 1485 but mystery and disagreement surround many of the issues and events connected with his death. The precise location of his grave is not known and there are several possibilities for its original site. Various traditions exist relating to the subsequent fate of his remains, whilst recently even the location of the battlefield on which he lost his life has become a matter for dispute.

Richard had been on the throne for just two years when he was killed in combat at the Battle of Bosworth on 22nd August 1485. Afterwards his naked and bloody corpse was slung over a horse and brought back to Leicester, where it was displayed for several days in the Collegiate Church in the Newarke, not least to dispel any doubts that he was definitely dead.

Some historians believe that Richard's remains were subsequently interred at Leicester Abbey, but the most widely accepted story is that his body was handed over to the Grey Friars who were given permission for its burial in their church in the medieval part of Leicester. Ten years later, whilst Henry VII was passing through Leicester, he ordered a monument to be erected there to Richard. Walter Hilton, an alabasterman from Nottingham was involved in its construction and the cost was £50. Little is known of its appearance though, except that it included a likeness of the late King, and may (according to a nineteenth century source) have had a rather unflattering inscription which in translation ran:

> "I WHO AM LAID BENEATH THIS MARBLE STONE,
> RICHARD THE THIRD, POSSESSED THE BRITISH THRONE,
> MY COUNTRY'S GUARDIAN IN MY NEPHEW'S CLAIM,
> BY TRUST BETRAY'D, I TO THE KINGDOM CAME.
> TWO YEARS AND SIXTY DAYS, SAVE TWO, I REIGN'D;
> AND BRAVELY STROVE IN FIGHT, BUT, UNSUSTAIN'D;
> MY ENGLISH LEFT ME IN THE LUCKLESS FIELD,
> WHERE I TO HENRY'S ARMS WAS FORC'D TO YIELD.
> TH'YEAR FOURTEEN HUNDRED 'TWAS AND EIGHTY-FOUR,
> THE TWENTY-FIRST OF AUGUST, WHEN ITS POWER
> AND ALL ITS RIGHTS I DID TO THE RED ROSE RESTORE.
> YET AT HIS COST MY CORSE THIS TOMB OBTAINS,
> WHO PIOUSLY INTERR'D ME, AND ORDAINS
> THAT REGAL HONOURS WAIT A KING'S REMAINS.
> READER, WHO'ER THOU ART, THY PRAYERS BESTOW,
> TO ATONE MY CRIMES, AND EASE MY PAINS BELOW."

The monument was probably destroyed shortly after the Friary was suppressed by Henry VIII in 1538. As to the fate of Richard's remains, popular belief claims that his bones were rudely disinterred and thrown off the western end of Bow Bridge into the River Soar. Over three centuries later, when the old bridge was demolished in 1862, a male skeleton was found embedded in the river mud. A Dr Lancaster took charge of the find, and later that year, it was examined at a meeting of the local archaeological and historical society. The skeleton was found to be that of a person aged between thirty and forty, and although there was damage to the cranium, the evidence was insufficient to conclude that the remains were those of the King.

Bow Bridge Leicester where plaques both on the bridge itself and on an adjacent wall commemorate Richard III

An alternative story suggests that Richard's bones were not left to lie in the river but were hastily collected up out of the water and re-interred without a coffin in the burial place of the Augustinian Friars on the west side of Bow Bridge. The current wall plaque near the bridge supports either theory. Richard's original stone coffin was said to have been used for many years as a drinking trough for horses outside the now-vanished White Horse Inn in Leicester's Gallowtree Gate. Later, its remaining broken fragments were reputedly used to repair the building's cellar steps towards the end of the eighteenth century. However, a second stone coffin also said to be associated with the King is still in existence.

Other sources suggest that Richard's bones were never disinterred from Grey Friars. In 1612, Christopher Wren's father came to Leicester to visit Robert Herrick, whose house was built on part of the site of the ruined Franciscan Friary. Wren later recorded seeing in the garden a three feet high stone pillar, which Herrick had erected, and upon which was inscribed:

"HERE LIES THE BODY OF RICHARD III SOME TIME KING OF ENGLAND".

If this is correct, then unless disturbed later, Richard's remains must now lie somewhere in the area around New Street, Grey Friars and St. Martin's Cathedral, the most likely location being beneath a private car park on the west side of New Street. Herrick's pillar has long gone, and for many years the supposed site of the King's grave lay completely unmarked until recently, when a fund was successfully launched to raise money for a fitting tribute. With little remaining of the Friary, St. Martins being both the Parish Church and Cathedral was chosen as the most appropriate site for the memorial stone. Carved by David Kindersley and bearing Richard's crown and coat of arms, it was set into the chancel floor and dedicated in August 1982. Its inscription reads:

"RICHARD III KING OF ENGLAND KILLED AT BOSWORTH FIELD IN THIS COUNTY 22ND AUGUST 1485 BURIED IN THE CHURCH OF THE GREY FRIARS IN THIS PARISH."

In October 1990 a further memorial to Richard III was inaugurated in Leicester by the Duke of Gloucester. Located on the National Westminster Bank in St. Martins, it depicts the King's burial at nearby Grey Friars, his emblem and his motto. Additional local memorials and sites connected with Richard III are to be found elsewhere in Leicester, in Sutton Cheney Parish Church, and at the Battlefield of Bosworth site.

Cairn at Bosworth Battlefield, erected in 1813, above the well where Richard III is said to have drank before the Battle

Richard's reputation suffered considerably under the succeeding Tudor dynasty who were anxious to assert the legitimacy of their right to rule. Shakespeare's play also reinforced his image as a sinister, humpbacked, monstrous ruler. More recent historians have partly redressed the balance, and today Richard III's abilities are more widely acknowledged and his reputation partially improved.

A notice in the churchyard of St. James the Greater at Dadlington tells how in 1511, Henry VIII founded a charity there for the souls of those killed at the Battle of Bosworth. Many of the slain are believed to be buried there, which may explain the large number of unmarked grave mounds clearly visible all over the churchyard. Not far away, a communal grave for some of the battle casualties is thought to exist just north of St. James' at Sutton Cheney. It is this church, where according to tradition Richard III attended his last mass.

Sir Thomas Berkeley (d.1488)
Wymondham, St. Peter

Geoffrey Sherard (d.1492)
Stapleford, St. Mary Magdalene

Sir John Digby (d.1533)
Melton Mowbray, St. Mary

Wars of the Roses

Amongst the local figures caught up in the Wars of the Roses are three whose memorials are all to be found in the north-eastern part of the county. Sir Thomas Berkeley and Geoffrey Sherard were two of the local Commissioners of Array. The third was Sir John Digby, a Lancastrian supporter who distinguished himself on the Battlefield of Bosworth.

Sir Thomas is commemorated at Wymondham by a tomb-chest which now stands in the south transept close to the recumbent effigy of a fourteenth century crusader. The monument used to have a finely incised alabaster top, but most of the carving has been worn away and replaced by a selection of graffiti added by later generations. Sir Thomas served as a Justice of the Peace under Edward IV, Richard III and Henry VII, and for several years filled the positions of Sheriff for Rutland, Warwickshire and Leicestershire.

Detail from Geoffrey Sherard's brass, Stapleford St. Mary Magdalene. The figures represent his seven sons and seven daughters

A short distance away, in a secluded position within the grounds of Stapleford Park, is the Church of St. Mary Magdalene. It is a notable building with an outstanding series of monuments to the Sherard family. Geoffrey Sherard's well-preserved brass in the middle of the nave floor is the oldest of these. It shows him in a suit of armour, with a shield behind his back and a greyhound at his feet. His wife is by his side. Below is a row of smaller figures which represent their fourteen children. As happened to some of the other memorials here, Geoffrey Sherard's brass was removed from the old medieval church at Stapleford to the "new" church during the eighteenth century. Whilst there, it is also worth looking in the church gallery to see the Sherard family pew, complete with its own Adam fireplace. The hall itself has recently been converted to a luxury hotel.

John Digby was a hero of Bosworth field. He fought on the winning side and was suitably rewarded for his efforts by gifts of local land from the new king. Later, he received a knighthood. He also became a King's Marshall, but after failing in his duties by letting a group of prisoners escape, he resigned the post on payment of a forfeit. Afterwards he served as an officer at Calais and took part in the Low Countries Wars under Henry VIII. He retired to Ab Kettleby and when he died his remains were interred in the south aisle of St. Mary's at Melton Mowbray. The Digbys are also commemorated at Sherborne in Dorset and Coleshill in Warwickshire, as well as at Stoke Dry, Ab Kettleby, North Luffenham and Tilton-on-the-Hill in Leicestershire. A tomb at Tilton was once believed to be that of Sir Everard Digby, knighted by James I in 1603 at Belvoir, and executed not long afterwards for his part in the Gunpowder Plot.

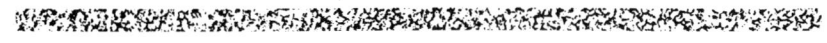

Cardinal Thomas Wolsey (c.1475-1530)
Leicester Abbey

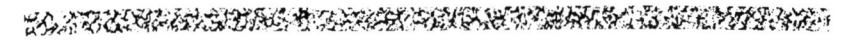

Henry VIII's most powerful minister

In Leicester's Abbey Park, amidst the low walls which mark the site of what was once one of England's largest Augustinian abbeys, is a flat memorial slab surrounded by low chains. It bears the name of a famous Tudor statesman accompanied by a quotation from Shakespeare's "King Henry VIII":

"CARDINAL
WOLSEY
OBIT A D 1530
GIVE HIM A LITTLE EARTH
FOR CHARITY."

Wolsey was the son of an Ipswich butcher. He served as chaplain to Henry VII and went on to become one of the most powerful and influential ministers at the court of King Henry VIII. For almost fourteen years his position was impregnable and at the height of his power he is said to have outshone even Henry VIII in magnificence. Proudly regarding himself as an equal of kings, Wolsey began to behave like one. He used a golden seat, a golden cushion and a golden cloth on his table, and when he went out on foot, he had his cardinal's hat carried before him and raised aloft like a holy idol. Arrogant, ambitious, and worldly, he was also a great statesman and diplomat of outstanding ability.

Wolsey's fall came in 1529 after his failure to obtain the Pope's approval of Henry VIII's divorce from Catherine of Aragon. Forced to resign, he reluctantly left court and went north. By autumn 1530, much to the government's concern, he was steadily regaining strength and power. A date was set for his enthronement as Archbishop of York, and there were rumours that he had persuaded the Pope to agree to excommunicate the King. Wolsey soon found himself arrested and ordered to London to answer charges of high treason. As he approached the Midlands his health rapidly failed, and on reaching Leicester Abbey, he is said to have told the Abbot "Father . . .I am come to lay my bones among you." There he was honourably received and taken to a chamber where he lay fitfully for the next three days. On the 29th November. at eight o'clock in the morning he died and early the following day he was interred in the Lady Chapel of the Abbey Church. A superb sarcophagus of black marble with four great pillars of bronze and a gilded bronze likeness which Henry VIII had planned for him was never finished. The associated unused coffin was later placed in Jane Seymour's grave, before being adapted eventually for Nelson's tomb in St. Paul's crypt.

A few years after Wolsey's death, the Crown Commissioner arrived at Leicester and closed down the Abbey. Afterwards the whereabouts of Wolsey's tomb and monument (if any) became uncertain. Various attempts were made later to discover it. Well-known Leicester dilettante and musician William Gardiner (q.v.) was involved in several unsuccessful efforts, including one on behalf of a phrenologist who had offered two hundred guineas for the Cardinal's skull. The antiquarian Browne Willis and others also searched without success. One story however tells that the supposed coffin was found by a gardener of the Countess of Devonshire, but he was ordered to cover it back up immediately, and as far as is known the coffin is still buried within the Abbey ruins.

John Farnham (c.1515-1587)
Quorn, St. Bartholomew

Thomas Farnham (1527-1562)
Stoughton, St. Mary and All Saints

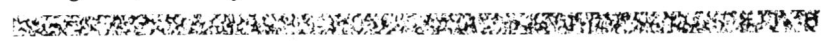

royal officials from a prominent Leicestershire family

An interesting feature of St. Bartholomew's, Quorn is the Farnham family chapel which is one of the few remaining private chapels situated within a parish church. Behind its closed off arches in the south aisle are numerous monuments to members of the Farnham family. Prominently placed in the centre of the chapel is a large ornamented table tomb which originally stood in the north aisle. It commemorates John Farnham (d.1587) and his wife Dorothy, whose effigies lie on top with superbly carved beasts at their feet. Farnham was an official to the royal stables under King Henry VIII, and later through the patronage of the Duke of Norfolk became M.P. for Steyning.

Up until the end of the nineteenth century, the chapel in St. Bartholomew's north aisle was like the south, a private chapel. It was originally used as a family chapel by the Nether Hall branch of the Farnhams, and later after their line died out as a chapel for the tenants of the Quorn Farnhams.

The Farnham family also have connections with St. Mary's at Stoughton where a prominent alabaster tomb at the west end of the church commemorates John's brother Thomas. Thomas was a Teller of the Exchequer during Queen Mary's reign, an esquire of the body at Queen Elizabeth I's coronation, and afterwards holder of the profitable position of Clerk of Liveries in the Court of Wards. Between 1553 and 1559 he was successively M.P. for Leicester, East Grinstead and Gatton. His granddaughter married Sir Thomas Richardson, Speaker of the House of Commons in one of Charles I's parliaments.

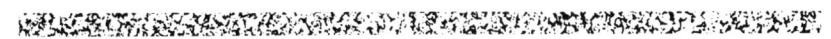

Thomas Corbett (d.1586)
Nailstone, All Saints

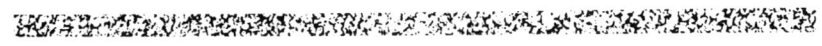

at ninety-four, the oldest official at court

If the Tudor court had given medals for long service, then Thomas Corbett would certainly have been eligible. He served Henry VIII, Edward

151

VI and both Queen Mary and Queen Elizabeth, eventually becoming the oldest official at court. He died at the age of ninety-four and was buried at All Saints' Nailstone. Of his tomb, only the marble top remains. This was rescued from beneath a stone by a former rector and can now be seen near the altar, fixed upright against a wall. On it is the outline of a man in a slashed doublet and ermine collar. His hair is short and he sports a long pointed beard. The now faded inscription is worth quoting at length:

> HEARE LYES ONE THOMAS CORBETT BY NAME
> WHOSE VIRTUES RARE DUE SHINE
> IN ALMES TO POORE, GOOD WILL TO RICHE
> NONE COULD CHARGE HIM WITH.
>
> KING HENRY TH'EIGHT HIS SERVANTS SURE
> IN PANTRY'S RULE DID BEARE
> KING HENRY, HIS WIVES AND CHILDREN THREE
> HE SERVED FULL THREESCORE YEAR.
>
> THE ELDEST OFICER IN THE COURT
> OF AGE NYNETY-FOURE YEARS
> THE SEAS HE PAST, THEIRE TO FULFILL
> THE KING HIS LORD'S AFFAIRS.
>
> AT CORONATIONS FOURE HE WAS
> AND CHIEF IN PANTRY THERE
> TO WAIT UPON THE PRINCES' BORD
> SO COMELY WAS HIS CHEARS.
>
> NINETEEN CHILDREN ONE WIFE TO HIM
> BROUGHT FORTH IN EIGHTEEN YEARS
> AND TWO ALSO ANOTHER WIFE
> TO HIS GREAT JOY DID BEARE.
>
> AND NOW HIS SOLE IS GIVE TO GOD
> HIS BONES LYE IN THIS GRAVE
> HOPING TO RISE WHEN GOD WILLS SO
> BY CHRIST HIS NEEDS TO HAVE.
>
> THE TWENTY THREE OF AUGUST MORNE
> IN THE YEAR DEPARTED HE
> A THOUSAND AND FIVE HUNDRED EKE
> WITH EIGHTY AND TWICE THREE.

Anthony Jenkinson (d.1611)
Teigh, Holy Trinity

the first Englishman to visit Central Asia

In an unmarked grave in the small Rutland village of Teigh, lie the remains of Anthony Jenkinson: a great English explorer, adventurer and diplomat. He is the first Englishman known to have penetrated Central Asia, and is one of only two people who have ever sailed the English flag on the Caspian Sea.

Jenkinson's travels belong to the phase of English exploration which aimed to end the Turkish and Italian monopoly of eastern trade by opening up a direct north-eastern route between England and the much fabled land of Cathay (China). Jenkinson was appointed Captain General of the Muscovy Company's Russian fleet in 1557, his task being to explore overland from Moscow eastwards to Cathay. Accordingly he set out from Gravesend on 12th May 1557, and sailed across the North Sea around the top of Scandinavia. He landed near Archangel and then headed south to Moscow. There the notorious Tsar Ivan the Terrible welcomed the party with lavish hospitality. The following spring, after the worst of the winter had passed, Jenkinson left Moscow. He worked his way down the River Volga and then sailed across the Caspian Sea. Back on land he joined up with a caravan of a thousand camels. Eventually he arrived in the Mongol city of Bukhara. Although his plans to push on further had to be abandoned, no Englishman had ever travelled this far east before. He arrived back in Moscow in September 1559 and on returning home the following year, produced a remarkable map of the journey. His mission not only did much to develop Anglo-Russian trade but also added greatly to western knowledge of Russia and the East, opening up the way for later exploration to India and beyond.

Afterwards he became involved in various undertakings and was for a while charged with preventing the Queen's enemy, Earl Boswell, from landing in Scotland. Later he retired to Northampton and died in 1611 at Teigh whilst visiting a friend.

Sir Richard Roberts (d.1644)
Church Langton, St. Peter

Civil War vandalism

Richard Roberts was a firm royalist ready to fight for his king even at the age of eighty. He died during the Civil War on 30th October 1644 and was buried at Church Langton. His mutilated effigy is to be seen in a recessed arch in the south aisle of St. Peter's Church. According to tradition, the missing feet and hands were cut off by roundhead soldiers shortly after the monument was erected about the time of the Battle of Naseby.

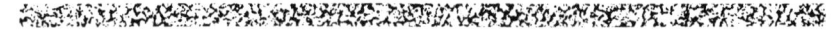

Sir William Herrick or Heyricke (1557?-1652)
Leicester, St. Martin

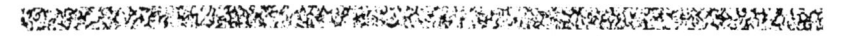

Elizabethan financier and royal jeweller

The Herrick family in America has strong ancestral links with Leicestershire. The first Herrick to go out to the "New World" is believed to have been Leicestershire born Henry Herrick, whose father Sir William Herrick lies buried in Leicester Cathedral. Sir William was a highly prominent goldsmith and banker. He also founded the Herrick estate at Beaumanor in Leicestershire.

Sir William Herrick (by permission of Leicestershire Museums)

Sir William came from a noted Leicester family. His elder brother Robert, his grandfather Thomas, and his uncle Nicholas all distinguished themselves in the administration of the town, holding between them most of the Borough's important positions during the Tudor period. William himself spent his boyhood in Leicester. As a teenager, he was sent to join his brother Nicholas' goldsmith business in London. Later he successfully set up on his own both as a goldsmith and financial dealer. His growing prosperity, talents, good looks and useful connections all helped further his progress. He acted as money-lender to Elizabeth I and later to James I. The Queen employed him as her ambassador to Turkey in 1581. Several years later he strengthened his links with Leicestershire by buying the Beaumanor estate from the discredited Earl of Essex. In 1601 he was made a Freeman of Leicester, promising the Mayor twelve silver spoons with cinque-foil knobs, instead of the usual fee of ten shillings. Not long afterwards he successfully stood as a parliamentary candidate for the town. Following the accession of James I, he became principal jeweller to the royal family and a Teller of the Exchequer, his services being rewarded by a knighthood in 1605. In later life however he was less in favour at the court of Charles I and during the Civil War his estate suffered considerably. Amongst many other noteworthy things, Sir William was a benefactor of Leicester's Trinity Hospital, and a guardian of the royalist poet, Robert Herrick.

St. Mary in the Elms at Woodhouse and the Cathedral in Leicester are the two main Leicestershire churches where members of the Herrick family are commemorated. Sir William's name can be seen on a centrally placed floor slab in St. Katherine's Chapel at the Cathedral, and also on a monument to the family at Woodhouse.

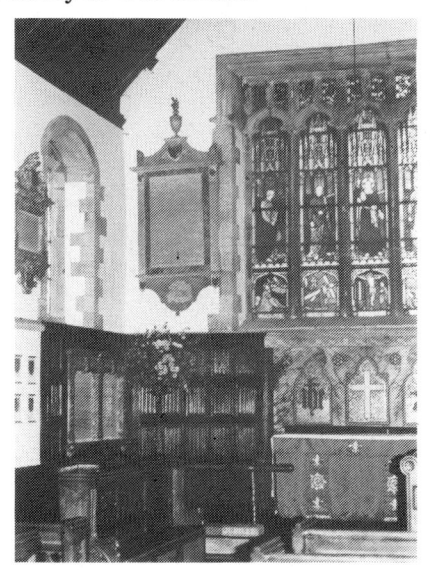

Interior of St. Mary in the Elms Woodhouse, where Sir William's career is recorded on the monument of one of his descendants

155

George Bathurst (d.1656)
Theddingworth, All Saints

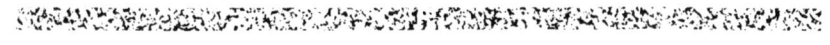

staunch royalists

Almost hidden behind the organ at Theddingworth is a fine wall memorial commemorating a staunch royalist family. Beneath the life-size oval portrait reliefs of George Bathurst and his wife is a row of small figures representing their thirteen sons and four daughters. Six of the boys died fighting for Charles I, another became chaplain to Charles II, and the youngest was treasurer to Queen Anne.

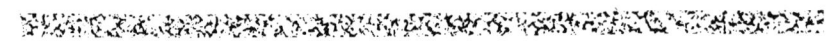

Sir Richard Halford (d.1658)
Wistow, St. Wistan

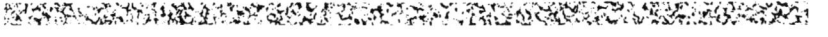

keeper of the king's saddles

Within easy reach of Leicester is Wistow where there is now a country park, a garden centre, craft shops and a tea room. A little way down the road towards Kibworth is a lake, beyond which is Wistow Hall, once home to generations of the Halford family. Standing alone amongst the trees on the opposite side of the road is the ancient church of St. Wistan. Of the many Halford family memorials to be found inside, the oldest is an armour-suited reclining figure in the north transept. It commemorates Sir Richard Halford, leader of the royalist cause in the area, who played host to King Charles I at Wistow on several occasions.

Just before the Civil War, Halford had been imprisoned in the Tower by the parliamentarians for declaring that the new M.P. for the Division Sir Arthur Hesilrige (q.v.), had more wit than wisdom. Made to kneel at the bar of the House and publicly recant, Halford was released from imprisonment upon payment of a large fine. A year later in 1641 Charles I created him a baronet in acknowledgement of his many loyal services to the Crown.

During the Civil War, Sir Richard's home at Wistow was a royalist stronghold. Charles I slept there on 4th June 1645 just before the Battle of Naseby, briefly returning with Prince Rupert ten days later. On their second visit, the royal party stopped off just long enough to change their brightly coloured crimson and gold saddles for something less conspicuous before fleeing northwards on fresh horses. The saddles and other equipment were never reclaimed and have been in the custody of Sir Richard and his successors ever since.

Sir Richard himself narrowly escaped execution during the Civil War and died peacefully in 1658. The inscription on his monument at Wistow says little about the Civil War however, and consists mainly of a lament for himself and his two sons, all of whom died within the space of two years. It also expresses concern for the uncertainty of the Halford family's future:

"WEEP NOT TO READ SO MANY WORTHIES DEAD,
BUT WEEP TO SEE SO FEW LEFT IN THEIR STEAD."

Detail from Sir Richard Halford's monument at Wistow

Sir Arthur Hesilrige (1601-1660/1)
Noseley, St. Mary's Chapel

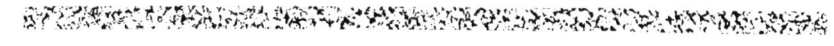

a former Leader of the House

Noseley Hall, home of the Hazlerigg family, lies tucked away amidst the beautiful rolling countryside of eastern Leicestershire. Within the grounds of the hall, close to the house, is the private family chapel. Amongst the chapel's interesting features are its unusual "cock pews" and several fine monuments. The prominent one near the altar with the row of children at its base, commemorates Sir Arthur Hesilrige, who spearheaded the local parliamentary cause during the Civil War and was once one of the most powerful men in England.

Hesilrige became an M.P. for Leicestershire in 1640, and soon made a name for himself as an outspoken critic of both the established church and the government of King Charles I. Two years later, he was one of the "Five Members" of Parliament whom King Charles personally, but unsuccessfully tried to arrest on a charge of treason. At the outbreak of the Civil War, Hesilrige fought as a general in the Parliamentary Army, distinguishing himself as head of his newly formed regiment of cuirassiers, nicknamed the "Lobsters" on account of their heavy iron armour and scarlet sashes. Between campaigns he took an active and increasingly important role in Parliament, becoming a leading member of the republican party. After Oliver Cromwell's death and the subsequent failure of Parliament under Cromwell's son Richard, Hesilrige's power reached its peak. He sat on all the important committees and was the recognised leader of the House for a while. At the Restoration however, he was arrested and sent to the Tower.

In his defence, Hesilrige declared that he had nothing to do with the late King's death and that he had only supported the Commonwealth to avoid bloodshed, remaining totally opposed to Cromwell's usurpation. Hesilrige was spared the scaffold, but died shortly afterwards in the Tower from fever. His remains were allowed to be taken to Noseley, where they were interred with great funerary pomp in the family chapel.

In an oval panel on Sir Arthur's monument is one of the several local inscriptions which recall the Civil War:

> "HERE LYES SIR ARTHUR HESILRIGE BARONT: WHO INJOYED HIS PORTION OF THIS LIFE IN YE TIMES OF GREATEST CIVILL TROUBLES YT EVER THIS NATION HAD. HE WAS A LOVER OF LIBERTY & FAITHFULL TO HIS COUNTRY HE DELIGHTED IN SOBER COMPANY AND DEPARTED THIS LIFE 7TH OF JANUARY IN ENGLANDS PEACEABLE YEAR ANNO DOM: 1660."

Below are the figures of Sir Arthur, his two wives and his children, several of whom carry skulls to indicate that they died in infancy. Interestingly, Sir Arthur is not only shown here on his own monument, but is also featured as a young boy on the magnificently coloured monument to his parents a few yards away.

Detail from Sir Arthur Hesilrige's monument, Noseley Chapel

Colonel Francis Hacker (d.1660)
Stathern, St. Guthlac?

signatory of Charles I's execution order

When Charles I was brought to trial, he was placed into the custody of Colonels Huncks and Hacker, the latter an enthusiastic Leicestershire parliamentarian. During the trial Hacker was given the important job of guarding the King, being responsible for providing the daily escort to Westminster Hall, and for regulating the comings and goings of all visitors. After the King's fate had been decided, Hacker took receipt of the death warrant. He subsequently signed the execution order and on the day, stood amidst the black drapes of the platform, supervising the proceedings. During the succeeding Commonwealth, the death warrant was kept at Stathern Hall, Hacker's Leicestershire home.

As a parliamentarian, Hacker was the notable exception from an otherwise royalist family. At the outbreak of the Civil War he had been elected to the Leicestershire Militia, and subsequently spent much of his time fighting in the county, distinguishing himself defending Leicester in 1645. Taken prisoner on several occasions, he was regarded as quite a prize, the royalists making several unsuccessful attempts to bribe him to change sides. After Charles I's death, Hacker supported Cromwell, helping to fight unrest all over the country. Local figures that he helped arrest included Lord Grey of Groby and George Fox, leader of the Quakers. He also became one of Leicestershire's parliamentary representatives, but as he later admitted himself, he was no great speaker.

Following the Restoration, Hacker was arrested and thrown into the Tower on 5th July 1660. Shortly afterwards, during the Lords' debate about who was responsible for Charles I's death, it was revealed that he still had the death warrant in his possession. He was ordered to produce it, mainly as evidence against those whose names it contained. Hacker's wife, fearing the worst, tried to help but only made things worse, unfortunately bringing to light the actual execution order that her husband had signed. Although Hacker had not signed the original death warrant, the rest of the evidence against him was sufficient to see him found guilty of regicide.

Hacker was hanged at Tyburn on 19th October 1660. Afterwards his body was handed over to relatives for burial. Although some sources say that he was interred at St. Nicholas Cole Abbey, London, there is a strong local tradition that his remains were brought back to Stathern where they were interred just outside St. Guthlac's chancel door.

Henry Firebrace (1619-1690/1)
Stoke Golding, St. Margaret

"a very faithfull and serviceable man"

Henry Firebrace was a loyal and faithful royal servant who held various offices within the royal household of King Charles I. When the Civil War broke out, Firebrace naturally joined the King's cause. Later, after the defeat of the royalists at Newark he loyally followed his captive master around the country, attending him at Holmby Hall, Hampton Court and Carisbrooke Castle on the Isle of Wight. Whilst on the island, Firebrace helped mastermind several plots to free the King.

One plan required the King to squeeze out of his bedchamber window and slide down a rope to the waiting Firebrace who would then take him over the castle walls to freedom. The plan failed when the royal body refused to go through the small opening of the window! Firebrace's next scheme involved the King's exit through a backstairs window after removing the impeding bars. These were to be partially dissolved by nitric acid. Wax and clay were to be used to hide and temporarily bridge the gaps made in the bars, and the job was to be finished off with a file. The King, although enthusiastic at first, later abandoned the plan as impractical. Another unsuccessful idea from Firebrace was for the King to escape in disguise by swapping places with a visitor who would come supposedly seeking a cure for the King's Evil. Not surprisingly, suspicion of Firebrace's activities grew and he was dismissed by the King's captors. On the day before he was executed, the King requested that a secret message be conveyed to his son, the future Charles II, commending Firebrace to him as one who had been a person "very faithfull and serviceable . . . and fit to be employed and entrusted."

Firebrace's lengthy and easily missed Latin epitaph in the Lady Chapel of St. Margaret's Church, Stoke Golding, is one of the most interesting commentaries of seventeenth-century politics to be found in the county. According to the inscription, "after the arms of [the] rebels were victorious and tyranny imposed upon us", Firebrace retired to live in obscurity at Stoke Golding, "until, Heaven looking graciously upon the hopes of all men, Charles [i.e. Charles II] who was missed so much, returned to his own land". At the Restoration, Firebrace successfully petitioned to join the new royal household, where he was put in charge of private household affairs, and made one of the principal officers of the Green Cloth. The inscription continues, recalling how "With such integrity he lived for nearly 30 years at Court" and was ever dear to Charles II and James II "those august brothers". However on the accession of William of Orange, "in order to keep faith he returned to this familiar haven and former refuge".

Colonel William Cole (d. 1698)
Laughton, St. Luke

royalist from Laughton

Inside St. Luke's Church at Laughton is an almost square wall plaque, with a small circular heraldic brass inlay. It commemorates William Cole, a former lord of the manor, High Sheriff of Leicestershire and an active army officer. The inscription tells how for fifty-eight years he served "his Majestie King Charles the first of blessed memory, and ye three Kings his successors." Colonel Cole lived to be eighty-four dying on 27th March 1698. He left no male heir, but a later maternal descendant was the famous Leicestershire cricketer J.T. King.

John Shenton (1612-1699)
Barwell, St. Mary
(Also commemorated at Husbands Bosworth, All Saints)

hidden valuables in a moat at Barwell

John Shenton was a captain of the cavalry in the royalist army. He fought at the Battle of Worcester in 1642, escaping afterwards to his estate at Barwell. On hearing that a search party was out looking for him, he hid his valuables in the moat which surrounded his house, and himself in a large elm tree, later known as "The Spreading Tree" or "John Shenton's Tree". Its stump stood until recently on the Hinckley to Barwell road. Later he fought at Naseby and lived on to see both the Commonwealth and the Restoration. In the children's corner at Husbands Bosworth Church is a very attractive wall memorial which jointly commemorates John Shenton and a later member of the family, Austin Kirk Shenton who was killed at the Battle of Amiens in 1918. The memorial includes both their swords as well as two cannon balls from Naseby. John Shenton's burial place is however at Barwell.

John Smith (1656-1726)
Frolesworth, St. Nicholas

Baron of the Exchequer from Frolesworth

One of Frolesworth's most famous sons was the Honourable John Smith, a former student of Gray's Inn who became a Baron of the Exchequer in England, and afterwards Lord Chief Baron of Scotland. Throughout his life he remained much attached to Frolesworth, keeping a house there (reputed to be the White House), and when he died, left provision in his will to endow the village with an almshouse. This building, with some later additions and improvements, still stands on the corner opposite the Plough Inn, and is easily identified by a commemorative wall plaque. Further afield, Smith's endowments include the Church of St. Paul and St. George in Edinburgh. Visitors to Frolesworth can read more about him on a large upright slab set into the south wall of the chancel of St. Nicholas.

Sir Christopher Packe (1593-1682)
Prestwold, St. Andrew

Sir Gilbert Heathcote (1652-1733)
Normanton, St. Matthew
(Monument moved to Edith Weston, St. Mary)

two Lord Mayors of London

Of the people commemorated locally who made their names in the capital, two were former Lord Mayors of London. One was Sir Christopher Packe of Prestwold, the other Sir Gilbert Heathcote of Normanton. As expected, both have elaborate memorials. Sir Christopher's at Prestwold is a tall conspicuous monument, which shows him as a full length figure reclining on top of the base of the tomb, and dressed in his official robes and chains. Lower down on one of the side panels, and easily missed, are carvings of his mayoral mace, sword and hat. Similar symbols can also be found on Rysbrack's elegant wall memorial to Sir Gilbert Heathcote at Edith Weston.

appointed Mayor in "very difficult times"

Sir Christopher was a native of Kettering who made his fortune as a wool merchant in London. He was an influential member of the Drapers Company and a governor of the powerful Company of Merchant Adventurers. According to his Latin inscription at Prestwold, his appointment as Mayor was made in "very difficult times". Later as an M.P. for London, he sat in Oliver Cromwell's last parliament, and was amongst those who petitioned Cromwell to assume the title King. Not surprisingly, following the Restoration Sir Christopher fared badly. Disqualified permanently from holding public office, he quietly retired to his Leicestershire estate at Prestwold. He died there in May 1682 and was buried in the family vault beneath St. Andrew's chancel. The best time to visit the church is when the gardens of Prestwold Hall are open to the public.

founder of the Bank of England

Symbols of the office of Lord Mayor of London decorate Rysbrack's memorial to Sir Gilbert Heathcote, at Edith Weston St Mary

Sir Gilbert Heathcote was a highly successful financier and international trader, who acquired the reputation of being the richest commoner in England. He was also one of the founders of the Bank of England. However his wealth combined with a reputation for parsimony, made him an easy target for such commentators as Alexander Pope who wrote: "The grave Sir Gilbert holds it for a rule, that every man in want is nave or fool". In contrast, Sir Gilbert's epitaph at Edith Weston glows with praise:

"A PERSON OF GREAT NATURAL ENDOWMENTS, IMPROVED BY LONG EXPERIENCE, READY TO APPREHEND, SLOW TO DETERMINE, RESOLUTE TO ACT; A ZEALOUS FRIEND TO THE RIGHTS AND LIBERTYS OF MANKIND; IN OFFICES OF POWER AND TRUST, TRUE TO HIS OWN AND COUNTRY'S HONOUR; . . . A KIND LANDLORD, A STEADY FRIEND, AN AFFECTIONATE RELATION; IN HIS CHARACTER UNBLEMISHED . . . "

Four times an M.P., he was appointed Lord Mayor of London in 1711, reputedly governing with "Courage and Temper". Towards the end of his life he purchased the estate at Normanton, and when he died he was buried nearby at St. Matthew's. Over two centuries later when work started on Rutland Water the church was deconsecrated and his memorial moved to St. Mary's at Edith Weston, where it is now on display at the west end of the north aisle.

Not long after Sir Gilbert's death, one of his successors demolished Normanton village so that the estate could be enlarged, moving the villagers en masse to Empingham. Normanton Hall was demolished in 1925, its stones being re-used to construct the White House at Scraptoft. The Hall's stable block has survived and a hotel has recently been opened on the site.

Baron Lawrence Carter (1671-1744)
Leicester, St. Mary de Castro

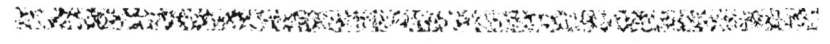

government legal advisor

Baron Carter (by permission of Leicestershire Museums)

St. Mary de Castro is where the young Henry VI was knighted in 1426. The church is also the location of a sizeable marble wall memorial to Baron Lawrence Carter, a prominent judge and successful lawyer who served as solicitor-general to the Prince of Wales, afterwards King George II.

Carter was in his mid-twenties when he succeeded Nathan Wright as Recorder for the Borough of Leicester in 1697. The next year, following in his father's footsteps, he became M.P. for Leicester. He later served as the Crown's Council during the Jacobite Rising in 1715, becoming Serjeant-at-law and King's Serjeant in 1724. This was followed by promotion to Baron of the Exchequer in 1726. In Leicester, five dozen bottles of wine and three and a half pounds of sweetmeats were ordered by the Mayor and aldermen to celebrate the event. Carter remained on the Exchequer Court bench until his death in March 1745. His remains were interred at St. Mary de Castro.

The house which he had built on the site of the Collegiate Church of the Annunciation in the once fashionable Newarke area of Leicester, stood until earlier this century when expansion of the Technical College necessitated its demolition. Dr William Watts (q.v.), founder of the Leicester Royal Infirmary, was his nephew.

John Manners, Marquis of Granby (1721-1770)
Originally buried Bottesford, St. Mary
(Later Belvoir Castle Mausoleum)

a famous soldier who added a new phrase to the English language

John Manners, Marquis of Granby, was one of the most popular soldiers in British history. Brave to a fault, honest, generous, hard-drinking and ever caring for the well-being of his soldiers, he was a brilliant cavalry leader, idolised by his men and highly regarded by the public.

His first commission was as a Colonel in Scotland during the Jacobite Rebellion. He next saw action in Flanders and by 1755 had become a Major-General. During the Seven Years War that followed, he was in Germany, succeeding Lord Sachville as Commander-in-Chief of the British forces there. By the end of the war in 1763, he had a long string of victories to his name. He had distinguished himself as the hero of the Battle of Minden in 1759, and during the following year had achieved his greatest triumph when he successfully led a spectacular cavalry charge against the French at the Battle of Warburg, resulting in 1,500 French losses. On that occasion, he is said to have charged with such speed and force that his wig flew off leaving him bald-headed. Unconcerned he dashed onwards, giving rise afterwards to the expression "to go for someone bald-headed".

In 1763, he returned to England to unbounded popularity, with messengers waiting at all the key ports of entry to offer him a choice of jobs. He accepted the post of Master General of the Ordnance and three years later was promoted to Commander-in-Chief of the entire British Army. Granby was also an M.P. representing Grantham from 1741 to 1754, and Cambridgeshire from 1754 until his death in 1770. He died at Scarborough from gout, and his death was greatly mourned throughout the country. William Pitt described his loss to England as "irreparable", and many other tributes followed. The body was brought back to Belvoir and interred at St. Mary's Bottesford, where it lay for almost half a century before being removed to the newly constructed mausoleum at Belvoir Castle. Although there is no memorial to the Marquis at St. Mary's, the church houses a fine series of monuments to other members of the Manners family.

Granby's popularity is reflected in the many inns all over England which bear his name. Many of these were originally set up by his own soldiers on retirement from the service. His name also features in place names. Granby Street and the Granby Halls in Leicester are believed to be named after him. There were also verses, songs and a battle march written in his honour. His portrait by Sir Joshua Reynolds is currently on display at Belvoir Castle as are other items connected with his life. The Castle is also the home of the 17th/21st Lancers Regimental Museum.

John Manners, Marquis of Granby, c.1759 (by permission of the National Portrait Gallery, London)

10. Trades and occupations

Loughborough Tradespeople
Loughborough, All Saints

carpenter, hatter, cabinet-maker, currier

Gravestones which allude to a person's occupation can be particularly rewarding to find, especially those which mention bygone crafts and trades. Some have brief factual inscriptions, others full-blown rhyming verses, occasionally accompanied by illustrations of the tools of the trade.

The most extensive collection of such memorials in Leicestershire is at All Saints' Loughborough. There on the stones now lined up around the churchyard are the names of occupations such as mat-maker, edgetool maker, postmaster, carpenter, ironmonger, butcher, trumpeter, hatter, grocer, draper, plumber, innkeeper, cabinet-maker, carrier, apothecary, horse-dealer, currier, maltster and many more.

Other examples are to be found throughout the county.

Edward Baradell (d.1759)
Sileby, St. Mary

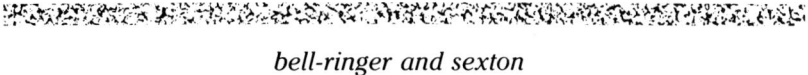

bell-ringer and sexton

Sexton Edward Baradell's finely carved slate in Sileby churchyard

Edward Baradell was Sileby's bell-ringer and sexton for over fifty years, and as such must have witnessed the burials of many local people. His own gravestone stands in Sileby's churchyard on a slight embankment just to the right of the main path leading towards the church, its inscription typical of eighteenth century tombstone versification.

> "FOR FIFTY-TWO REVOLVING YEARS
> DEVOUTLY HE ATTENDED PRAY'RS
> WITH MELLOW VOICE AND SOLEMN KNELL
> HE SUNG THE PSALMS AND TOLL'D THE BELL
> BUT CRUEL DEATH SPOIL'D HIS LAST STAVE
> AND SENT THE SEXTON TO HIS GRAVE
> AND HIS DEAR WIFE, LOVING AND KIND
> STAY'D BUT A LITTLE WHILE BEHIND."

A carved relief of a bell can be found on bell-ringer John Orton's more recent slate in Stoney Stanton churchyard (1853).

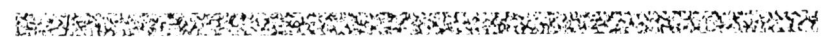

William Burton (d.1774)
Hinckley, St. Mary

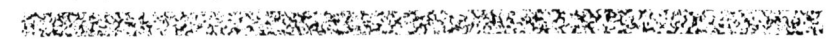

comedian and actor-manager

An unusual occupation is mentioned on a gravestone now set flat upon the grass near the entrance to St. Mary's churchyard:

> "HERE LIETH INTERRED THE BODY OF WILLIAM BURTON
> COMEDIAN
> WHO DEPARTED THIS LIFE MAY 2, 1774, IN THE 42ND YEAR OF HIS AGE."

The inscription has not fared so well as many of the others in the churchyard, and the last few lines which used to read:

> "SILENCE HOW DREAD AND DARKNESS HOW PROFOUND!
> TIS AS THE GENERAL PULSE OF LIFE STOOD STILL, AND NATURE MADE A PAUSE!
> AN AWFUL PAUSE! PROPHETIC OF HER END."

are no longer legible.

William Burton, a native of Norwich, was the talented actor-manager of a travelling theatre company which usually worked the main season at Margate and went out on the road during the rest of the year. In March 1774, he brought his troupe to Leicestershire to put on their show at Hinckley where he later died on 2nd May. Unlike some strolling players who acquired dubious reputations, he had apparently been known as a gentleman: "well behaved intelligent . . . and a lover of science." His daughter Elizabeth, also a talented performer, played for David Garrick's Drury Lane company.

Samuel Turner (1717-1784)
Market Harborough, St. Mary in Arden

William Hibbins (d.1785)
Ketton, St. Mary

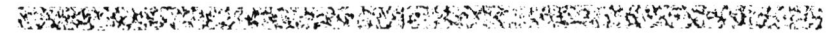

monumental masons

It is perhaps not surprising to find that some of the most interesting occupational headstones belong to monumental masons. Amongst Leicestershire's most talented masons were Samuel Turner of Market Harborough and the Hibbins family of Ketton.

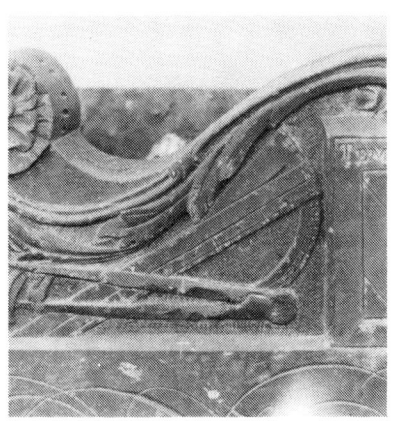

Survey instruments and an estate plan on Samuel Turner's gravestone, St. Mary in Arden Market Harborough

Samuel Turner's best known work is the illustrated autobiographical Swithland slate he carved for himself in 1782, barely two years before his death. It stands amidst the many interesting slates which are now lined up around the outside of the ruins of St. Mary in Arden at Market Harborough. Across the top of the stone and down each side runs a decorative border. The centre-piece of the top panel is a miniature sundial which used to have a metal gnomon. To the left are surveying instruments and an estate plan. To the right is a shepherd's hut and two sheep with a self-portrait of Turner at work in the corner. Halfway down the left hand panel is an artist's palette. The inscription tells how Turner was a shepherd up to the age of thirty-four when he took the decision to move to Market Harborough changing "the Cottage for the Shop and the Crook for the Pencil". He worked there for over thirty years, earning a living from surveying, painting and engraving. A number of churchyards in south Leicestershire and Northamptonshire contain good examples of his art. He was also responsible for producing the oldest map of Market Harborough, a copy of which is currently on display in the Harborough Museum.

Tools of the mason's trade at Ketton churchyard on William Hibbins' gravestone

The tools of the mason's trade, including dividers, a square, hammer, pick and chisel are carved in relief on the top part of master mason William Hibbins' gravestone. It is one of an impressive array of Ketton stones which now line the path between the lychgate and the entrance to St. Mary's at Ketton. Generations of the Hibbins family worked as masons in the area, and the extravagantly carved rococo styled memorials of Ketton stone that they produced are to be found in churchyards throughout Rutland and adjoining counties. "Hibbins House" on Ketton's High Street was built by the family for their own use and is a fascinating mixture of architectural ornament and styles. Not far away at Oakham, a collection of tools formerly used by the family is on display at the Rutland County Museum.

Thomas Holland (d.1786)
Twyford, St. Andrew

mole catcher

Thomas Holland of Twyford was a mole catcher who had a mole sculpted on his tombstone:

> *"at the top of an upright Swithland stone, in a hollow circle painted green, is sculptured a tomb, painted black, with a green cover, on the front of which is cut the word MOLE. The tomb is surmounted by an urn painted brown, the colours symbolical; the green signifying the grass-land, under which the mole generally burrows; the brown denoting the colour of the earth, in which the mole works, and from which it subsists; the tomb painted black, as in mourning for the deceased; the mole in its proper colour, black, shining, and inclining to a lead colour."* (John Nichols)

Although the colours have now gone, the stone can be found in St. Andrew's churchyard and there are descendants of Thomas Holland still living in Twyford today.

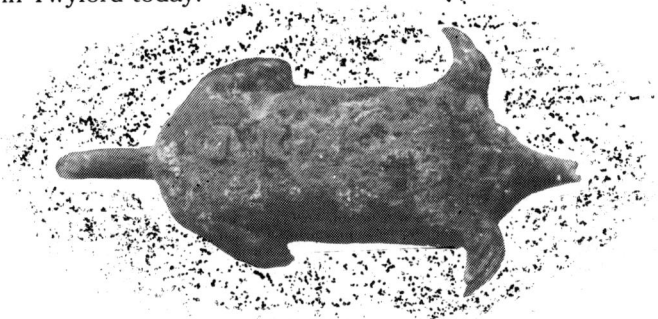

Carved mole on the gravestone of mole catcher Thomas Holland, Twyford St. Andrew

Samuel Marvin (d.1787)
Earl Shilton, St. Simon and St. Jude

a champion wrestler

From Earl Shilton comes an unusual epitaph to a once well-known wrestler:

> *"HERE LIE THE EARTHLY REMAINS OF SAMUEL MARVIN*
> *WHO IN HIS YOUTH WAS VIGOROUS AND ACTIVE,*
> *AND IN HIS MORE MATURE STATE BOLD AND UNDAUNTED.*
> *HE MUCH EXCELLED IN THAT MANLY AND ATHLETIC*
> *EXERCISE OF WRESTLING*
> *AND DIED JAN.17, 1787, AGED 49,*
> *IN PEACE WITH ALL MANKIND.*
> *AT LENGTH HE FALLS; THE LONG LONG CONQUEST'S O'ER,*
> *AND TIME HAS THROWN WHOM NON E'ER THREW BEFORE.*
> *'TIS HIS FIRST FALL: BEFORE NO MATCH WAS FOUND,*
> *BY SLIGHT OR STRENGTH TO FLING HIM TO THE GROUND;*
> *BUT HE SHALL RISE AGAIN, WITH YOUTH RENEW'D;*
> *TIME SHALL BE CONQUER'D AND THE GRAVE SUBDUED."*

Formerly on view near the church door, the stone is no longer there today, having probably been moved, damaged, or lost during restoration work.

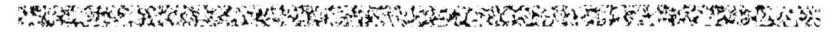

William Clark (d.1796)
South Kilworth, St. Nicholas

ingenious blacksmith

The tools and activities of the village blacksmith's craft, like those associated with wheelwrights, railwaymen and butchers, readily lent themselves to verse as William Clark's tombstone in South Kilworth churchyard testifies:

> *"ON THE DEATH OF AN INGENIOUS BLACKSMITH*
> *MY SLEDGE AND HAMMER LIE RECLIN'D,*
> *MY BELLOWS TO HAVE LOST THEIR WIND*
> *MY FIRE EXTINCT, MY FORGE DECAY'D*
> *MY VOICE WITHIN THE DUST IS LAID*
> *MY COALS ARE SPENT, MY IRON GONE,*
> *MY NAILS ARE DROVE, MY WORK IS DONE."*

These lines are said to have been written by the poet Hayley, and can be found in many other churchyards up and down the country.

Samuel Pears (d.1809)
Wymondham, St. Peter

rag and bone man

One of Leicestershire's most celebrated occupational headstones stands in the western part of St. Peter's churchyard at Wymondham. Its black painted inscription commemorates nonagenarian Samuel Pears, a rag and bone man by trade:

> "I IN MY TIME DID GATHER RAGS
> AND MANY A TIME I FILLD MY BAGS,
> AL-THO IT WAS A RAGGED TRADE
> MY RAGS ARE SOLD AND DEBTS ARE PAID.
> THEREFORE GO ON DONT WASTE YOUR TIME
> ON BAD BIOGRAPHY AND BITTER RHYME
> FOR WHAT I AM THIS CUMBROUS CLAY ASSURES
> AND WHAT I WAS IS NO AFFAIR OF YOURS."

The last four lines are somewhat curious especially as the deceased was reputedly quite a character.

Intriguing epitaph on Samuel Pears' tombstone, St. Peter's churchyard Wymondham

Joseph Smith (d.1826)
Leicester, St. Martin

a former Leicester Macebearer

Carved at the top of a gravestone near the entrance to St. Martin's churchyard, Leicester is the municipal cinque-foil emblem. Reading the inscription below, the reason for this becomes clear:

> "JOSEPH SMITH D. 16TH JANUARY 1826 AGED 77. HE HELD THE OFFICE OF MACEBEARER FOR THIS BOROUGH, AND DURING A PERIOD OF TWENTY FIVE YEARS DISCHARGED THE DUTIES OF THAT OFFICE WITH ZEAL AND FIDELITY."

The cinque-foil decorates macebearer Joseph Smith's headstone, St. Martin's Leicester

Joseph Smith was one of the last holders of the ancient office of Macebearer before the upheavals of 1836, when not long after his death, much of the town's pageantry was done away with, and the mace together with the Town Plate were sold off. During his period of office, the post carried with it an annual salary of £7 9s 8d. This was supplemented by an annual board allowance of £40 which had been introduced in 1801 when the Macebearer ceased to be entitled to board with the Mayor. Additional income came from acting as Inspector of the Corn Market, assisting the Borough Chamberlains, and from gratuities. In 1810 the Corporation received a petition for a pay increase from a number of its servants who felt that their increased responsibilities should be better rewarded. Although Smith was not one of the petitioners he came out of it £20 a year better off, on account of "the great zeal, diligence and fidelity" which he constantly showed whilst in the service of the Corporation!

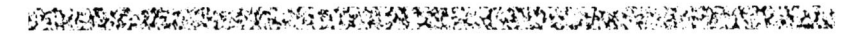

Rasselas Morjan (d.1839)
Wanlip, Our Lady and St. Nicholas

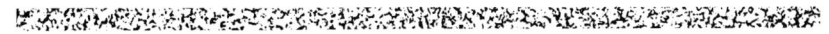

Wanlip servant "rescued from a state of slavery"

The gravestones of servants can often be found in churchyards close to large country houses. Their inscriptions reveal a fascinating array of occupations from whippers-in to gardeners, butlers, stewards and housekeepers. One of the most interesting collections of such stones is in the Vale of Belvoir in a clearing amongst the woods high up on the Harston to Woolsthorpe Road. Although just over the Lincolnshire border, the cemetery contains many memorials to former Belvoir Castle employees. In Leicestershire itself a number of churchyards in the Vale have similar memorials as do others in close proximity to larger country houses, for example at Exton, Breedon-on-the-Hill and Gumley.

In Wanlip churchyard, close to the path, is a mid-nineteenth century Egyptian-styled headstone. It commemorates Rasselas Morjan, a former slave, who briefly worked for the Palmers of Wanlip Hall.

"SACRED
TO THE MEMORY OF
RASSELAS MORJAN,
WHO WAS BORN AT MACADI,
ON THE CONFINES OF ABYSSINIA,
AND DIED AT WANLIP HALL,
AUGUST 25TH, 1839,
IN THE 19TH YEAR
OF HIS AGE.

RESCUED FROM A STATE OF SLAVERY
IN THIS LIFE
AND ENABLED BY GOD'S
GRACE TO BECOME A
MEMBER OF HIS CHURCH
HE RESTS HERE IN THE HOPE
OF A GREATER DELIVERANCE HEREAFTER.
THIS STONE IS RAISED
IN REMEMBRANCE OF HIS
BLAMELESS LIFE BY ONE
WHOM HE LOVED."

Although few other facts about Morjan's life are known, it is likely that he was "rescued from a state of slavery" by the Babingtons of Rothley Temple, a family well-known in the anti-slavery movement and close friends of the Palmers of Wanlip into whose care he was placed. Fleeting comments in contemporary letters from people staying at Wanlip Hall point to Morjan having become a uniformed servant there. In 1836 he was reported to be not only very well, but also very much pleased with another row of buttons on his clothes, a sign of promotion within the servant ranks. He was also able to read and was well liked by his fellow servants. A while later and much to the satisfaction of the Palmers, his christening took place at Wanlip, an event alluded to on his gravestone.

Exactly a century before Morjan's death, Giovanni Modena was buried in Shepshed churchyard. As can be seen from Giovanni's tombstone he too was from abroad and like Morjan had become a local servant: "A native of Linos one of the Islands in the Archipeligo & servant of Samuel Phillipps Esq."

Egyptian-styled headstone to a former slave in Wanlip churchyard

Thomas Ball (d.1857)
Sapcote, All Saints

"an honest and trustworthy labourer"

There are quite a few examples in Leicestershire of monuments erected by employers to former trusty employees, often inscribed with the names of both parties. From Thomas Ball's upright slate tombstone in the southern part of Sapcote churchyard it is learnt that he was "FOR MORE THAN 33 YEARS . . . AN HONEST AND TRUSTWORTHY LABOURER ON ONE FARM. HIS LAST EARTHLY MASTER: Wm. SPENCER: ERECTS THIS IN MEMORY OF ONE WHO ALWAYS TRIED TO DO HIS DUTY."

Thomas Hassall (d.1858)
Glenfield, St. Peter (Old Church)

principal quarry clerk

Sometimes a gravestone was erected by workmen as a mark of respect to a former colleague. At Glenfield, in a prominent position behind the railings surrounding the old church ruins is a tall granite stone to Thomas Hassall, a former employee at the Mountsorrel Quarry. Its fading inscription reads:

"IN
MEMORY OF
THO. HASSALL
FOR MANY YEARS PRINCIPAL
CLERK AT THE MOUNTSORREL QUARRY
WHO DIED DEC. 2ND 1858
AGED 44 YEARS.
THIS STONE WAS THE GIFT OF
THE QUARRYMEN OF MOUNTSORREL
AS A TOKEN OF THEIR REGARD
FOR THE DECEASED."

Walter Bates (d.1981)
Leicester, Gilroes Cemetery

"Proudly, a showman"

Occupational references on recent gravestones are relatively uncommon when compared with those of the eighteenth and nineteenth centuries.

However, one of the best contemporary examples can be found in Leicester's Gilroes Cemetery. This has a finely carved illustration of a fairground carousel and gallopers, accompanied by the inscription "Proudly, a showman". It commemorates the well-known Leicester showman Walter Bates, who for more than forty years helped to bring enjoyment to many all over the county with his family's travelling funfair. The fair was originally set up by his father earlier this century, before he took over the running of it in the 1950's. He also devoted considerable time and effort to charitable fund-raising and helping under-privileged groups. Very popular wherever he went, his death was regarded as a great loss by many in and around Leicester.

A fairground carousel decorates showman Walter Bates' memorial, Gilroes Cemetery Leicester

11. Connections

Sir Thomas Burton (1622-1659)
Stockerston, St. Peter

links with the "Arabian Nights"

Set into the floor at the east end of the south aisle of St. Peter's at Stockerston is a large flat dark grey stone. It records the death of Sir Thomas Burton, a cavalier who was once imprisoned in the Tower for his services to King Charles I. An old helmet, said to have been carried at Sir Thomas' funeral hangs high above on the adjacent wall. Several generations later the holder of the baronetcy died without heir.

Thomas Burton (1821-1890) the famous explorer and translator of "The Arabian Nights" is said to have had the right to the baronetcy but could not prove his claim. His own monument incidentally, is one of the most extraordinary in England, being a life-size stone tent in the churchyard of St. Mary Magdalen at Mortlake.

Stockerston church is a short distance from the village itself and is approached from a "no through road" which leads up to Stockerston Hall.

Heraldic display on Sir Thomas Burton's stone, Stockerston St. Peter

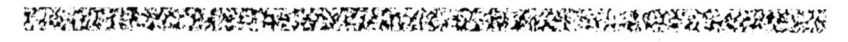

Abigail Swift, née Herrick (1640-1710)
Leicester, St. Martin

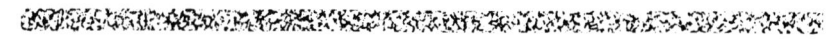

mother of Dean Swift

The trail of one of Leicestershire's most interesting literary connections can be picked up at St. Martin's Cathedral in Leicester. The Cathedral is the burial place of the Herricks, a prominent Leicestershire family, many of whom are commemorated in St. Katherine's Chapel in the north aisle (q.v. Sir William Herrick). Abigail Swift who is buried there was not only a Herrick but also mother of the famous writer Dean Swift, whose work includes the literary classic "Gulliver's Travels".

Both Wigston Magna and Houghton-on-the-Hill lay claim to being Abigail's birthplace, although Dublin where she is known to have met and married Dean Swift's father is more likely. Dean Swift himself was born and brought up in Dublin. On the death of her husband, Abigail left Ireland for England, coming to Leicestershire where she lived for the rest of her life. Later, Dean Swift also moved to England, working for a while for Sir William Temple at Moor Park near Farnham. He regularly visited his mother, usually travelling to Leicester on foot or in bad weather by carriers cart, staying at the cheapest and most obscure inns on the way.

When his mother died, Dean Swift was in Ireland. With uncharacteristic tenderness, he wrote in his diary:

> "... my dear mother Mrs. Abigail Swift dyed that morning, Monday April 29th, 1710, about ten o'clock, after a long sickness, being ill all winter and lame, and extremely ill a month or six weeks before her death. I have now lost my barrier between me and death, God grant I may live to be as well prepared for it, as I confidently believe her to have been. If the way to Heaven be through piety, truth, justice and charity she is there."

Further connections between Swift and Leicestershire are to be found in the county. It was at Frisby-on-the-Wreake where his uncle was the parson, that he nearly married Esther Vanhomrigh. Nearer to Leicester, he was a frequent guest of Sir George Beaumont at Stoughton Grange, often enlivening conversation at the dinner table with his wit and sarcasm. He is also believed to have written part of the inscription on the monument to Sir George inside Stoughton Church. Swift himself was buried at St. Patrick's Cathedral, Dublin.

Mary Powell (d.1794)
Bitteswell, St. Mary

Twinings Tea Company

In the north-east part of St. Mary's churchyard next to the church itself, is a large chest tomb enclosed by railings. On one side of the monument is the name Mary Powell, wife of the Reverend James Powell, vicar of Bitteswell, and "daughter of Mr Twining of London". Mary's family were the same Twinings who founded the celebrated London tea company in the eighteenth century, her father being an early manager of the firm.

Following Mary's death at the age of twenty-three in 1794, the Reverend Powell was left with their small daughter to look after. Concerned about the girl's future in the event of his own death, he had a house built for her in what was then the vicarage grounds at Bitteswell. Known as "The Lodge", the house was also used by other members of the Twining family, the last to live there being Richard Twining (q.v.).

There are monumental inscriptions to the Twinings inside St. Mary's Church, as well as a further memorial to Mary Powell near to the altar.

Sarah Crabbe (1751-1813)
Muston, St. John the Baptist

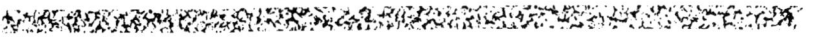

wife of a famous poet

A simple tablet at Muston records the death of Sarah Crabbe, wife of the poet George Crabbe. The couple met at Woodbridge in Suffolk where Crabbe was apprenticed to a local doctor. Later Crabbe abandoned the medical profession in favour of writing poetry, supported (on Edmund Burke's advice) by a career in the church. In 1782 he came to Leicestershire as chaplain to the Duke of Rutland and in the following year he and Sarah were married. Their first child was born at Belvoir. In 1785 Crabbe was appointed curate of Stathern and later he became rector of Muston. Besides poetry, he was particularly interested in botany. He cultivated a number of rare plants at Muston as well as contributing botanical information to John Nichols' "History and antiquities of the County of Leicester".

Sarah died in 1813, the deaths of five of their seven children having taken their toll on her health. She was buried at Muston and it is said that Crabbe was so distraught by her death that he asked for the grave to be kept open for himself. He eventually recovered, and following his death in 1832 was buried at Trowbridge in Wiltshire.

White marble memorial to Sarah Crabbe, Muston St. John the Baptist

Annie Elizabeth Greatorex (1865-1866)
Knighton, St. Mary Magdalene

a living memorial

Two varieties of cooking apples with Leicestershire connections are "Dumelow's Seedling" and "Annie Elizabeth". The first, also known as the "Wellington", was introduced by Dumelow, a Shackerstone farmer, whilst the "Annie Elizabeth" has its origins closer to Leicester. This was raised by Samuel Greatorex in what is now the Avenue Road area of Knighton, and was named after his daughter Annie Elizabeth Greatorex, who sadly died in infancy and is buried in Knighton churchyard.

Originally a seedling of the "Blenheim Orange", the "Annie Elizabeth" received a first class certificate from the Royal Horticultural Society in 1868, and was introduced commercially by Harrison's of Leicester about 1898. Very popular with gardeners, it bears heavy fruit which keeps well, is resistant to frost, and makes a good show apple.

William Turner (1792-1867)
Birstall, St. James the Greater

Augusta Ada King, Countess of Lovelace (1815-1852)
Commemorated at Kirkby Mallory, All Saints

outswam by Lord Byron

Two Leicestershire churches possess memorials which have links with the famous poet Lord Byron.

The first, a brass memorial to British diplomat William Turner, in the chancel of the older part of St. James the Greater, Birstall, is an unlikely connection through swimming. Lord Byron was a good swimmer, and in 1810 whilst on his first grand tour of Europe, he successfully swam the strait of water known as the Dardanelles which separates Europe and Asia. Ten years later, William Turner decided to emulate Byron's achievement but failed, and in trying to justify the result, found himself engaged in correspondence with Byron. Turner maintained that to swim from Asia to Europe as he had attempted, was far more difficult than to swim as Byron had from Europe to Asia.

Turner spent much of his working life in the Middle East. In 1824 he married Mary Anne Mansfield, daughter of Leicester M.P. John Mansfield of Birstall House. The bride was given away by the future British Prime Minister, George Canning. Afterwards, on arriving in Constantinople, Mrs Turner is said to have caused a great stir amongst the local populace by the cut of her dress. In 1829, her husband was appointed envoy extraordinary and minister plenipotentiary to the republic of Columbia. Nine years later he retired from the service. He died at Leamington on 10th January 1867 and was interred at Birstall six days later.

Byron's computational daughter

The second connection with Byron involves one of the most impressive and unusual churchyard memorials in Leicestershire. A tall elaborate Victorian Gothic shrine stands in a railed off enclosure just beyond the normal line of the churchyard at All Saints' Kirkby Mallory. On it is the name of Byron's only daughter, Augusta Ada, Countess of Lovelace.

Her mother Anne Isabella Milbanke, a descendant of the Noel family and heiress of the Wentworth baronetcy, had married Byron in 1815. At the time, Byron was at the height of his fame, a darling of society and the object of much female attention. Lady Anne had hoped that marriage would reform him. She was wrong though, and shortly after the birth of their daughter (Augusta) Ada, she was driven by desperation to seek refuge for herself and the baby at her father's estate at Kirkby Mallory. It was from there that she wrote to Byron, emphatically saying that she would never return to him. Not long afterwards, Byron went to live in Italy, where he spent most of the remaining years of his life. Although Byron last saw Ada when she was less than a year old, she is mentioned in several of his poems, including "Childe Harold" and "Fare thee well". In 1821 a lock of her hair was sent to him at Pisa. She was married in 1835 to William Lord King who afterwards was made the Earl of Lovelace.

Ada is also remembered as a friend and colleague of Charles Babbage, the inventor of the first automatic calculating machine embodying the principles of digital computers. Not only was she a talented mathematician, but she was subsequently credited with being the world's first computer programmer. Latterly a computer programming language has been named ADA in her honour. This has been the mandatory programming language for nearly all United States military projects since 1984, and for N.A.T.O. work since 1986.

Ada is commemorated at Newstead Abbey as well as Kirkby Mallory, although her actual burial place is with her father at Hucknall in Nottinghamshire.

Gothic shrine to Lord Byron's only daughter in the corner of Kirkby Mallory churchyard

Robert Burnaby (1828-1878)
Loughborough, Emmanuel

a British Columbian town named after a Leicestershire settler

From a quick glance off the Nanpantan Road, Emmanuel churchyard at Loughborough looks almost devoid of gravestones. Outside the east end of the church however, is a cross on a stepped base which is of considerable interest, especially to Canadians. The more recently erected plaque on the church wall behind helps explain why. The cross and plaque both commemorate Robert Burnaby, a native of Leicestershire who settled as a pioneer in western Canada. He was a public servant and later a businessman after whom the present day town of Burnaby in British Columbia is named. The plaque at Emmanuel was unveiled by William Lewarne, Mayor of Burnaby, during a visit to Loughborough in July 1987.

Colonel Henry Horatio Kitchener (1805-1894)
Cossington, All Saints

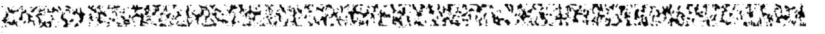

Lord Kitchener's father

Colonel Kitchener, who was the father of the celebrated national hero Lord Kitchener, came to live at Cossington in the early 1880's and when he died was buried in the local churchyard. The Colonel's grave lies just outside the east window of All Saints. Around the sides of the granite tombstone is the inscription:

> "LIEUT. COLONEL HENRY HORATIO KITCHENER LATE OF
> XIII LIGHT DRAGOONS AND IX REGIMENT.
> BORN 22 OCT. 1805 DIED 14 AUGUST 1894."

Lord Kitchener's visits to see his father aroused great interest amongst the villagers of both Cossington and nearby Rothley. Affectionate recollections tell how his tall figure would be seen walking the lanes to Rothley where his sister lived at Rothley Temple, and how after having been wounded during the Egyptian War, he would attend church services at All Saints' with his arm in a sling.

Lord Kitchener last visited Cossington for his father's funeral. Afterwards, having no wish to keep the Manor House, he tried to sell it off within the week, until tactfully advised by a Leicester auctioneer that he would get a better price by being a little more patient.

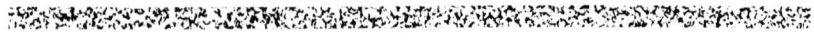

Fisher Family
Higham-on-the-Hill, St. Peter

a well-known Archbishop of Canterbury's family

In the south-east corner of Higham-on-the-Hill churchyard is a tall cross on a stepped base, commemorating the Fisher family. Their most distinguished member was Geoffrey Francis Fisher, born at Higham in 1887, who became Archbishop of Canterbury and Primate of All England in 1945. Under his leadership, the Church embarked on a wide-ranging programme of reform, including pastoral reorganisation and revision of the Canon Law. He presided at the coronation of Elizabeth II, and became the first Archbishop of Canterbury since the Reformation to visit Rome for a papal meeting. Archbishop Fisher himself is buried in the churchyard at Trent near Sherborne in Dorset.

The Fisher Window at St. Helen's Church, Ashby-de-la-Zouch provides a further link with the family.

Taft Family
Chataway Family
Peckleton, St. Mary Magdalene

an ancestor of a United States President and relatives of a well-known athlete

At St. Mary Magdalene at Peckleton are two unexpected connections. One is with a United States President; the other with a famous sporting achievement.

In the eastern part of the churchyard, close to the huge yew tree, is the grave of a Taft. He was a distant ancestor of William Howard Taft, the twenty-seventh President of the United States of America.

In the same churchyard, are memorials to the Chataway family. These commemorate relatives of the well-known athlete Chris Chataway, who helped to set the pace for Roger Bannister in his record-breaking mile run of less than four minutes, at Oxford in 1954.

The eastern section of Peckleton churchyard

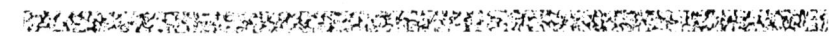

Sir Raymond Greene (1869-1947)
Commemorated at Burrough-on-the-Hill, St. Mary

famous Greene connections

Distinguished army officer, politician and keen huntsman Sir Raymond Greene, whose memorial is in the south aisle of St. Mary's Burrough-on-the-Hill, was the grandson of the founder of the Greene King Brewery in East Anglia. He was also a relative of the novelist Graham Greene. As an M.P., Sir Raymond represented the Chesterton division of Cambridgeshire from 1895 to 1906 and North Hackney from 1910 to 1923. He also served as a member of the London County Council. Later, after resigning his seat, he moved from Suffolk to Burrough, bringing his staff with him. He lived at Burrough House for many years, enjoying the convenience of the location for hunting. Following his death in 1947, he was cremated and his ashes spread over the rockery in the garden by his butler using a silver spoon from the house. Sir Raymond's patriotism and his enthusiasm for hunting are both reflected in his epitaph at Burrough:

*"ENGLAND AND FRIENDS HE LOVED DEARLY
AND THE JOY OF HIS LIFE WAS A HORSE".*

A Guide to Sources

During the course of researching this book several hundred site visits were made and numerous sources were used. A vast amount of the biographical information was gleaned from material in the Leicestershire Collection and Humanities Library at the Information Centre, Bishop Street, Leicester. Additionally, a great many records and other sources relating to burials, gravestones, monuments and inscriptions were also consulted. The following brief guide is included as a research aid to some of the main Leicestershire sources.

Burial Records and Registers

The obligation on parishes to keep records of burials dates back to 1538 and although generally few parish registers have survived from this time, a substantial proportion of Leicestershire's Anglican burial registers date from the latter part of the sixteenth century. Entries in the earlier registers are invariably brief, giving little information other than name and date of burial. Occasionally, additional details such as occupation or marital status are given. As well as their content, these early registers also vary considerably in size, arrangement and legibility. In 1813 however, a standardised format was introduced. This not only means that entries after this date are much easier and quicker to read, but also makes the records more useful for family history purposes by including information on both the age and the "abode" of the deceased.

Related records include Bishops' Transcripts which were copies made of the Anglican registers. These can help to provide information where the original register has not survived or is incomplete.

Not all burials in Anglican graveyards were recorded, and for some periods the register is more accurately a record of funerals which took place with Anglican rites, rather than a complete record of burials. Those who did not receive an Anglican burial, or for whom no burial service was performed, will generally not be recorded there. It is also possible for a burial to be "missing" simply because the officiating clergyman forgot to record it.

Not everyone was buried in Anglican ground and increasingly from the eighteenth century onwards, other religious groups often founded and used their own burial grounds. However, they were not under compulsion to keep any registers until the middle of the nineteenth century.

A great many burial registers have now been deposited at the Leicestershire Record Office where microfiche copies of the originals are readily available. A smaller number are still in the keeping of the church or chapel concerned, as of course are registers which are still current. A list is available from Leicestershire Record Office of all the registers which have been deposited there. Microfiche copies of many of these registers are also available in certain Leicestershire libraries.

Cemeteries and Crematoria

During the nineteenth century, overcrowding in churchyards led to the establishment of burial grounds which were not attached to a church or chapel.

In Leicester the first such public burial ground to be opened was the Welford Road Cemetery. Originally intended as a private burial ground for the Dissenters, the project was taken over by the Corporation as a public work, and on 19th June 1849, the Mayor of Leicester, William Biggs, (brother of John Biggs q.v.), laid the first stone. The first interment took place just over a week later. Part of the 17 acre site was left unconsecrated for use by the Dissenters, with the remainder being consecrated for Church of England use. There were also two chapels, one for each group, since demolished in the late 1950's. By 1894, the size of the cemetery had been extended to 30 acres and 112,892 burials had taken place, of which more than two-thirds were in the unconsecrated section. Today, many worthies and leading families of Leicester lie within its grounds, their imposing monuments lined up along the paths and terraces. Other cemeteries were subsequently opened throughout the county and cremation facilities first became available in Leicestershire in 1902.

Cemetery records are usually extremely well kept and extensively detailed. They include a daily register of burials, grave registers showing ownership and listing those buried there, locations or grave numbers, site plans, information on monuments and alphabetical indexes by name. Cremation records provide similar information including details of the disposal of ashes.

In Leicestershire the majority of these records are kept by the appropriate District Council. Initial enquiries are best made by letter or telephone, since these offices do not usually have the same facilities as public search rooms. An important exception is for the records of the Welford Road Cemetery Leicester, the majority of which have been filmed and are readily available on microfiche at the Leicestershire Record Office.

In addition to the cemeteries listed here, there are many others within each district that are administered by Parish or Town Councils.

Perimeter path at Leicester's Welford Road Cemetery which leads up to the south-eastern section where many of Leicester's worthies lie

CEMETERY RECORDS

AUTHORITY RESPONSIBLE	ADDRESS WHERE RECORDS ARE KEPT	CEMETERY	DATE OPENED	DATE RECORDS START
Charnwood Borough Council	Cemeteries & Crematorium Office Macaulay House 5 Cattle Market Loughborough	Loughborough	1857	September 1857
		Hathern	1896	March 1896
		Thurcaston (Managed by Charnwood B.C. on behalf of Hathern, Cropston & Thurcaston Parish Council's)	1934	September 1934
Harborough District Council	District Secretary's Dept. Council Offices Adam and Eve Street Market Harborough	Market Harborough (Harborough D.C. also hold burial records for Great Bowden and Saddington cemeteries and for Great Easton cemetery extension)	1878	?
Hinckley & Bosworth Borough Council	Ashby Road Cemetery Hinckley	Barwell	1899?	November 1899
		Earl Shilton	1929	August 1929
		Hinckley (Hinckley & Bosworth B.C. also hold burial records for Stoke Golding cemetery)	1858	April 1858
Leicester City Council	Recreation & Arts Dept. New Walk Centre Welford Place Leicester	Belgrave	1881	1881
		Leicester Gilroes	1902	1902
		Leicester Saffron Hill	1931	1931
		Leicester Welford Road	1849	See below
	Leicestershire Record Office 57 New Walk Leicester	The following records are deposited by Leicester City Council on indefinite loan in the Leicestershire Record Office where they are available on microfiche:		
		Leicester Welford Road:	1849-1953 Registers Consecrated Section 1849-1947 Registers Unconsecrated Section 1849-1943 Indexes	

(Leicestershire Family History Society also have microfiche copies of these.)

190

Melton Borough Council	Treasurers Dept. Council Offices Nottingham Road Melton Mowbray	Melton Mowbray	1893	June 1893
North West Leicestershire District Council	Technical Services Dept. Council Offices Whitwick Road Coalville	Coalville London Road Coalville Broom Leys Hugglescote Whitwick	1859 1927 1908 1878	1859 1927 1908 1878
Oadby & Wigston Borough Council	Council Offices Station Road Wigston	Oadby Wigston	1863 1882	August 1863 August 1882
Rutland District Council	For Information contact Council Offices Catmose Street Oakham	Oakham	1860	?

Note: There are no cemeteries under the control of Blaby District Council except the following closed burial grounds which the Council maintains: St. John the Baptist, Aldeby, Enderby; All Saints' churchyard, Blaby; St. Peter's churchyard, Whetstone; All Saints' churchyard, Sapcote and St. Michael's churchyard extension, Stoney Stanton.

CREMATORIUM RECORDS

Charnwood Borough Council	Cemeteries & Crematorium Office Macaulay House 5 Cattle Market Loughborough	Loughborough	1960	July 1960
Leicester City Council	Recreation & Arts Dept. New Walk Centre Welford Place Leicester	Leicester Gilroes	1902	1902

191

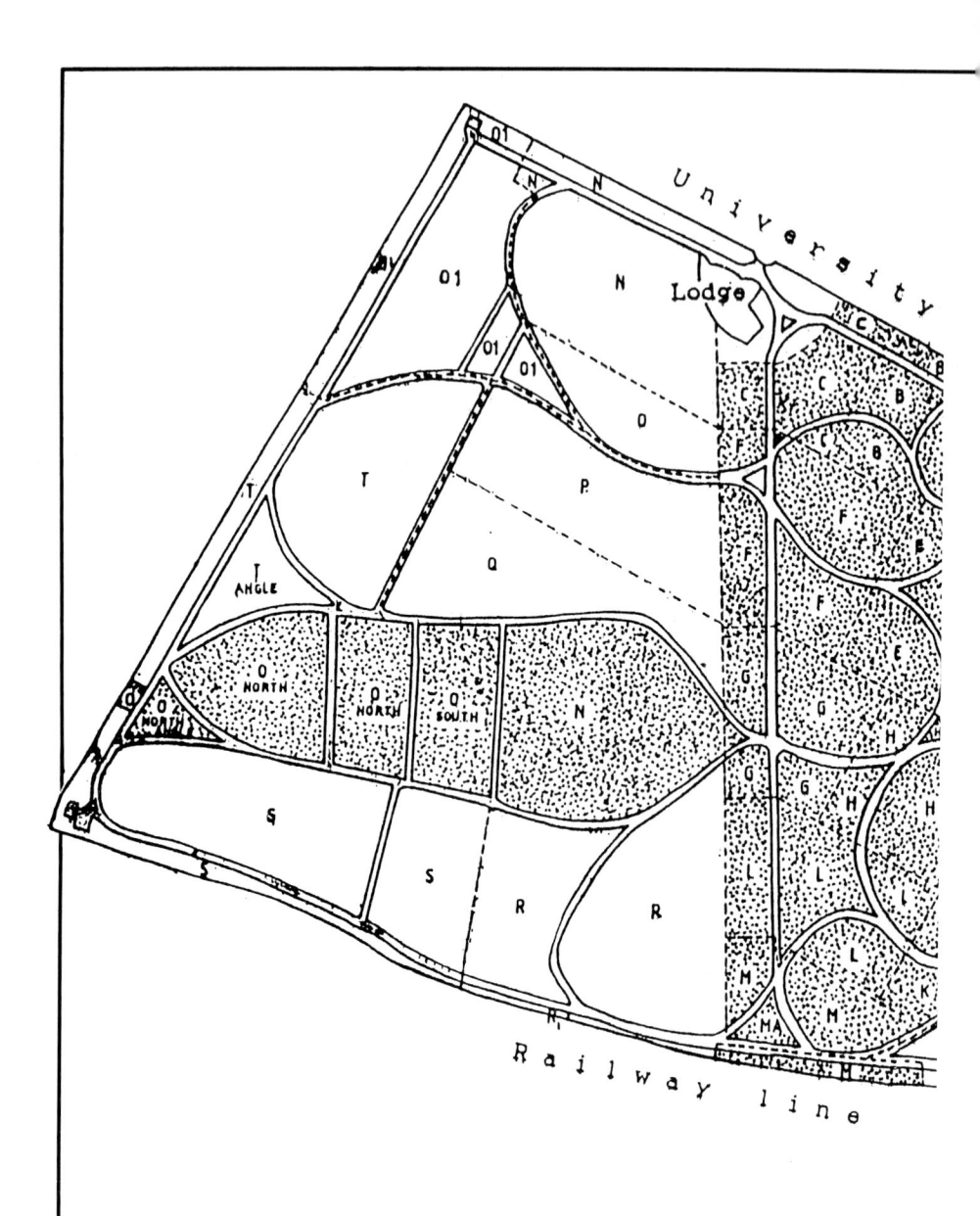

Plan of the Welford Road Cemetery Leicester (derived from an original from Leicester City Council Cemetery & Crematorium Dept and annotated by C.E.J. Aston, by permission of Leicestershire Record Office)

WELFORD ROAD CEMETERY LEICESTER

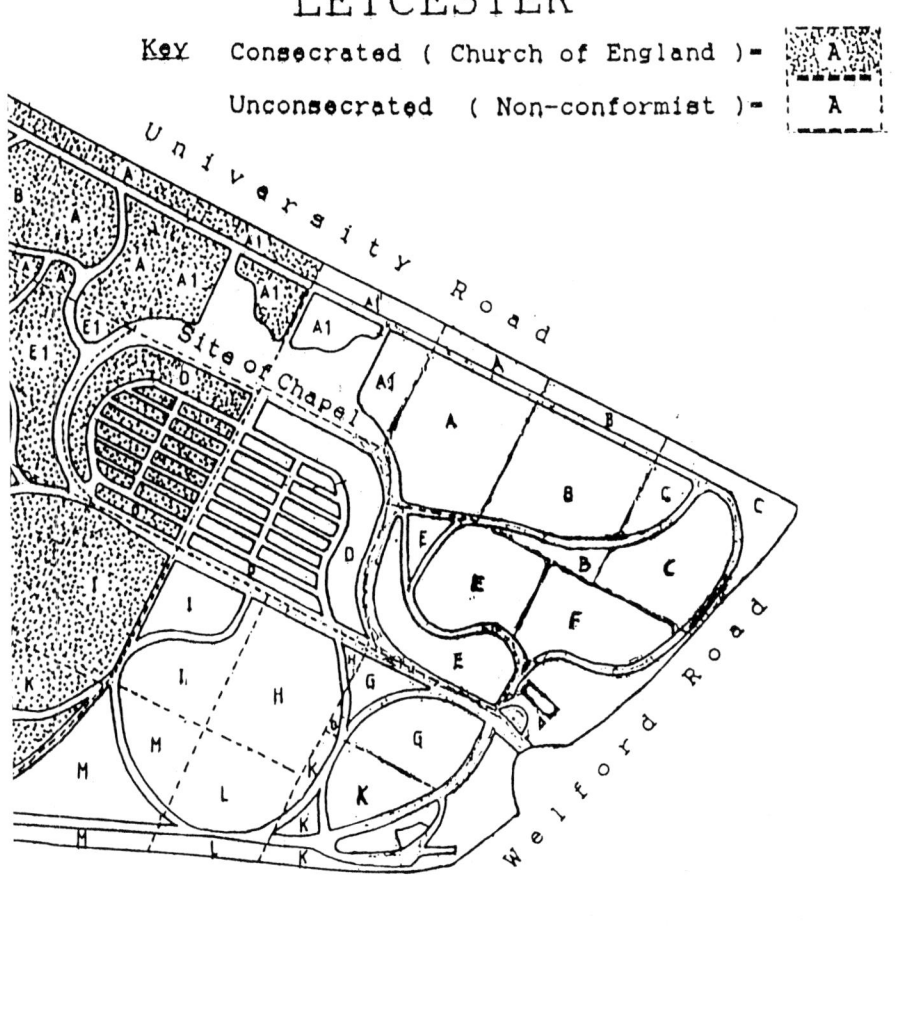

Key Consecrated (Church of England) — A
        Unconsecrated (Non-conformist) — A

Indexes to Burials and Other Sources

Official records sometimes include alphabetical name indexes to interments in a particular cemetery or burial ground. Alternatively, indexed transcripts of burial registers may be available. Even so, trying to find out where someone is buried can be a time-consuming task, particularly in the more populous urban areas, or where the date of death is not known. Especially useful therefore, are projects of the type currently being undertaken by the Leicestershire Family History Society, whose members are in the process of compiling a combined alphabetical name index to burials in Leicester from 1813 onwards. A major part of this project is the mammoth task of indexing the Welford Road Cemetery registers, initially for the period from 1849 to 1900. The index also includes burials at the churches of St. Margaret, St. Nicholas, St. George, All Saints and St. Martin. Members of the Leicestershire Family History Society are also compiling a list of all the burial grounds in the county.

Other useful sources of information include: wills which may give instructions for funeral and burial arrangements; national death indexes and death certificates (these do not however give the place of burial); church graveyard records; undertaker's records; notices of deaths, obituaries and funeral reports in newspapers and journals. These, together with the many other, often unexpected records, which can provide interesting information about a person on their death are discussed in more detail in publications such as "The Family Tree Detective" by Colin Rogers (1985) and "Family Forbears" by Jerome Farrell (1987).

Gravestones, Monuments and Inscriptions

Where a monument or gravestone exists, it may provide information not readily available elsewhere about the person commemorated and their relationships with others. Older monumental inscriptions tend to be more detailed than their modern counterparts. In some cases these can include not only an outline family tree for several generations, but also a potted eulogistic biography of the deceased, information on the cause of death, and a "helpful" or admonitory message for the reader.

The value of monumental inscriptions for historical and genealogical purposes has long been recognised, and considerable effort has gone into recording them. Consequently, the often lengthy task of locating monuments, gravestones and burial sites can be helped by consulting work which has already been carried out. For most purposes, the surveys of monumental inscriptions in individual graveyards will be the most useful. Details recorded include either a full transcript or an abstract of each inscription. There may also be a description or an illustration of the monument, a plan to show its location, and an index to all the names in the survey. These surveys can help to identify burials omitted from Anglican registers, whilst the older ones may also include information about stones which have subsequently been lost, damaged or badly weathered.

A great many graveyard surveys have been compiled for Leicestershire, the most comprehensive collections being held by the Leicestershire Record Office and the Leicestershire Family History Society. Lists of holdings are available from both.

One of the most extensive countrywide surveys ever, was carried out during the early 1980's by members of the Leicestershire and Rutland Federation of Women's Institutes. The results provide an extremely useful and well illustrated record of a large number of the county's outdoor monuments and gravestones. Surveys completed by the Women's Institute to date include the following:

Allexton	Frisby-on-the-Wreake	Rothley
Anstey	Gilmorton	Saddington
Appleby Magna	Glenfield	Sapcote
Arnesby	Glooston	Scalford
Arnesby (Baptist)	Groby	Scalford (Methodist)
Asfordby	Harby	Scraptoft
Ashwell	Hathern*	Sharnford
Bagworth	Higham-on-the-Hill	Shearsby
Barkby	Hoby	Sheepy Magna
Barrow-upon-Soar	Houghton-on-the-Hill	Slawston
Belton-in-Rutland	Husbands Bosworth	Somerby
Billesdon	Kibworth	South Kilworth
Bitteswell	Kilby	South Luffenham*
Blaby	Kirkby Mallory	Sproxton
Braunstone*	Leire	Stapleton
Broughton Astley	Lubenham	Sutton Cheney
Burbage	Market Bosworth	Swinford & Catthorpe
Burrough-on-the-Hill	Medbourne	Theddingworth
Burton Lazars	Morcott*	Thornton
Burton Overy	Narborough	Thrussington*
Burton Overy (U. Ref)	Newtown Linford	Thurcaston
Castle Donington	North Kilworth	Thurlaston
Copt Oak	Oadby	Thurnby & Bushby
Cottesmore	Oakham	Waltham-on-the-Wolds
Countesthorpe	Oaks-in-Charnwood*	Walton-le-Wolds*
Croft	Peatling Magna	Wardley
Cropston Cemetery	Queniborough	Whetstone
Dadlington	Quorn	Whissendine
Dunton Bassett	Quorn (Baptist)	Willoughby Waterleys
Elmesthorpe	Ragdale	Wistow
Empingham	Ratby	Woodhouse
Fenny Drayton	Rearsby	Wymeswold
Foxton	Ridlington & Preston*	
Foxton (Baptist)	Rotherby	

All are Church of England unless otherwise stated. Copies of these surveys, except those marked with an asterisk, have been deposited at the Leicestershire Record Office.

For interior monuments of the eighteenth century and earlier, John Nichols' "History and antiquities of the County of Leicester" (1795-1815) is the most comprehensive work for the old county of Leicestershire. A selection of churchyard memorials is also included. A more recent survey was carried out by Colin Ellis during the 1950's and 1960's. His manuscript records from these visits are now preserved at the Leicestershire Record Office. They include:

A card index to monuments inside Leicester churches, giving description, location, material, lettering, special features and maker's name for each monument, and a complete transcription of the inscription. There are approximately 1,000 cards arranged by church. L.R.O. Ref: 3D66/1.

A series of rough notebooks recording similar information for monuments inside Leicestershire churches, with an index of places included in each volume. L.R.O Ref: 3D66/2/1-28.

"Journals of a churchgoer", being Ellis' personal account of many of his visits. L.R.O. Ref: 3D66/3/1-3.

Detailed descriptions of the medieval incised slabs of Leicestershire (flat memorials which were originally laid on the church floor and later placed on the top of altar tombs), will be found in F. A. Greenhill's "Incised slabs of Leicestershire and Rutland" (1958). Nikolaus Pevsner's "Buildings of England: Leicestershire and Rutland" (1984) also pays considerable attention to the architectural and sculptural qualities of the more notable church monuments.

Additional information on monuments may be obtainable from the archives of monumental masons, individual parishes, and local authorities. Parish records sometimes report details of proposals and funding for memorials amongst the Parochial Church Council minutes. Also included are faculties for the erection, relocation, and restoration of monuments and occasional other interesting pieces of information.

Further helpful sources include the wide variety of individual church guide-books, village histories and local history journals that are available, and of course the knowledge and recollections of clergy, church-wardens, residents, local historians and many others.

Select Bibliography

BAILEY, Brian. *Churchyards of England and Wales.* Robert Hale, 1987
BAILEY, Brian. *Portrait of Leicestershire.* Robert Hale, 1977
BENNETT, J.D. *Who was who in Leicestershire 1500-1970.* Book House, 1975
BOASE, Frederic. *Modern English biography.* Frank Cass. 6 vols. 1965 (Reprint of 1892-1921 ed.)
BOOTH, Charles. *Life and labour of the people in London.* First Series: Poverty. Streets & population classified. Macmillan, 1902 (Reprint of 1891 ed.)
BURGESS, Frederick. *English churchyard memorials.* S.P.C.K., 1979
BURGESS, Frederick. Swithland slate carvers. English sepulchral monuments. *The Monumental Journal.* 1954-1957
CHILD, Mark. *Discovering churchyards.* Shire, 1982
COLLINSON, Hugh. *Country monuments.* David & Charles, 1975
COOK, Herbert W. *Worthies of Loughborough and district.* (MS)
CREAGH, Sir O'Moore and HUMPHRIS, E.M. *The V.C. and D.S.O.* Standard Art Book Co. 3 vols. 1924
Crockford's Clerical Directory
Dictionary of National Biography
ELLIS, Colin D.B. *Catalogue of local portraits.* Leicester Museums and Art Gallery, 1956
FARRELL, Jerome. *Family forbears.* Leicestershire Museums, Art Galleries and Records Service, 1987
FIRTH, J.B. *Highways and byways in Leicestershire.* Macmillan, 1926
FLETCHER, Rev. William George Dimock. *Leicestershire pedigrees and royal descents.* Clarke and Hodgson, 1887
GARDINER, William. *Music and friends.* Combe and Crossley; Crossley and Clarke. 3 vols. 1838-1853
Gentleman's Magazine, 1732-1829
GREENHILL, F.A. *The incised slabs of Leicestershire and Rutland.* Leicestershire Archaeological and Historical Society, 1958
GREENWOOD, Douglas. *Who's buried where in England.* Constable, 1982
HAWKER, James. *A Victorian poacher.* Edited by Garth Christian. Oxford University Press, 1961
HERBERT, Albert. *Swithland slate headstones.* W. Thornley & Son, 1945
HOSKINS, W.G. *A Shell guide: Leicestershire.* Faber and Faber, 1970
Illustrated London News, 1843-
KEMP, Brian. *Church monuments.* Shire, 1985
Leicester and Nottingham Journal, 1759-1786. Continued as *Leicester Journal,* 1787-1920
Leicester Chronicle, 1812-1979
Leicester Mail, 1910-1931. Continued as *Leicester Evening Mail,* 1931-1963
Leicester Mercury, 1874-
Leicestershire and Rutland Notes and Queries, 1891-1895
Leicestershire Archaeological and Historical Society Transactions

LINDLEY, Kenneth. *Of graves and epitaphs*. Hutchinson, 1965
MEE, Arthur. *The King's England: Leicestershire and Rutland*. Hodder and Stoughton, 1966
Modern memorials: Leicester. F. Hewitt, 1875 (Leicester University Library Local pamphlets)
NICHOLS, John. *The history and antiquities of the County of Leicester*. Originally published J. Nichols 1795-1815. 1971 Reprint S.R. Publishers in association with Leicestershire County Council.
Notes and Queries, 1849-
ORMOND, Richard and ROGERS, Malcolm. *Dictionary of British portraiture*. Batsford. 4 vols. 1979-1981
PALMER, Roy. *The folklore of Leicestershire and Rutland*. Sycamore Press, 1985
PARSONS, David, editor. *A bibliography of Leicestershire churches*. University of Leicester, Department of Adult Education. 1978-1984
PEVSNER, Nikolaus. *The buildings of England: Leicestershire and Rutland*. 2nd ed. Penguin, 1984
PIKE, W.T. editor. *Contemporary biographies*, in *Leicestershire and Rutland at the opening of the twentieth century*, by W. Scarff. W.T. Pike, 1902.
RAFTERY, Michael. *The writers of Leicestershire*. Leicestershire Libraries and Information Service, 1984
RAMSEY, D.A. *The Leicestershire slate industry*. Leicestershire Libraries and Information Service, 1985
Records of the Borough of Leicester, 1509-1835
Register of the George Cross. This England, 1985
Register of the Victoria Cross. This England, 1981
RILEY, H.G. compiler. *Some worthies born in Leicestershire*, in *The historical pageant of Leicestershire official souvenir*, edited by F. Shakespeare Herne. Pageant Committee, 1932
ROGERS, Colin. *The family tree detective*. 2nd ed. Manchester University Press, 1985
Rutland Magazine and County Historical Record, 1903-1912
Rutland Record, 1980-
SILVESTER, W.F. *Eighteenth century headstones in the Vale of Belvoir*. 1979 (MS)
TACEY, O.C. Swithland slates. *Bulletin of the Loughborough & District Archaeological Society*. 1973 Autumn 2 (1)
THROSBY, John. *Select views in Leicestershire*. J. Nichols, 1789
THROSBY, John. *Supplementary volume to the Leicestershire Views*. J. Nichols, 1790
The Times
VALENTINE, Dora C. compiler. *Church brasses of Leicestershire*. University of Leicester, Department of Adult Education, 1975
VESEY-FITZGERALD, Brian. *Gypsies of Britain*. David & Charles, 1973
Victoria history of the County of Leicester
WAITES, Bryan, editor. *Who was who in Rutland*. Rutland Record Society, 1987

Wallace's Local Chronology. William Wallace, 1927

WEATHERLEY, W. Samuel. *A description of the tombs and monuments having sculptured effigies up to the close of the seventeenth century*: with a digression upon the Swithland local headstones of the seventeenth and eighteenth centuries, in *Memorials of old Leicestershire*, edited by Alice Dryden. George Allen & Sons, 1911

Who Was Who

Wyvern, 1891-1899. Continued as *Leicester Guardian*, 1899-1906

YUNG, K.K. compiler. *National Portrait Gallery: complete illustrated catalogue 1856-1979*. National Portrait Gallery. 1981

Individual *church guide-books, village histories, local history journals, biographies* and *autobiographies*

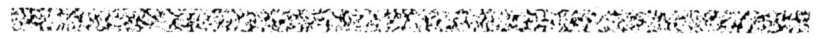

Gazetteer

Places, churches, cemeteries, burial grounds and people mentioned in the text. Page references are given in the Index.

ASHBY-DE-LA-ZOUCH
Ashby-de-la-Zouch Cemetery: Edward Mammatt
St. Helen: Selina Hastings – Countess of Huntingdon, Dr Thomas Kirkland, Edward Mammatt, John Prior

ASHWELL
St. Mary: Reverend James Williams Adams

BARROW-UPON-SOAR
Holy Trinity: Henry Barsby, Theophilus Cave, John Sydney Crossley, Joseph Taylor

BARTON-IN-THE-BEANS
General Baptist Chapel: Samuel Deacon

BARWELL
St. Mary: John Shenton

BELGRAVE
Belgrave Cemetery: Joseph Cave

BELTON-IN-RUTLAND
St. Peter: Robert Swann

BELVOIR
Belvoir Castle Mausoleum: Lady Diana Cooper, John Manners – Marquis of Granby
Belvoir Priory: Robert de Roos

BIRSTALL
St. James the Greater: William Turner

BISBROOKE
St. John the Baptist: Nathaniel Clark

BITTESWELL
St. Mary: Mary Powell, Richard Twining

BLABY
All Saints: Reverend Edward Stokes

BLASTON
St. Giles: Reverend Humfrey Michel

BOTTESFORD
St. Mary: Francis Manners – 6th Earl of Rutland, John Manners – Marquis of Granby, Robert de Roos

BRAUNSTONE
St. Peter: Richard Parsons

BREEDON-ON-THE-HILL
St. Mary and St. Hardulph: John Johnson

BURROUGH-ON-THE-HILL
St. Mary: Sir Raymond Greene

BURTON LAZARS
St. James: Wiliam Squire, Morpeth Webb, Count Luigi Zborowski, Count William Elliott Zborowski

CARLTON CURLIEU
St. Mary: Reverend William Fenwicke

CASTLE DONINGTON
St. Edward King and Martyr: Ferdinando Hastings

CHURCH LANGTON
St. Peter: Reverend William Hanbury, Sir Richard Roberts, Thomas Stavelie

COLEORTON
St. Mary: Sir George Howland Beaumont

CONGERSTONE
Congerstone Heath: John Massey

COSSINGTON
All Saints: Colonel Henry Horatio Kitchener

COSTON
St. Andrew: Temple Crozier

COTTESMORE
St. Nicholas: "Uncle" Edward Chapman Clayton

CROXTON KERRIAL
Croxton Abbey: King John

DISHLEY
All Saints: Robert Bakewell

EARL SHILTON
St. Simon and St. Jude: Samuel Marvin

EASTWELL
St. Michael: Reverend Edward Bullen

EDITH WESTON
St. Mary: Sir Gilbert Heathcote

EDMONDTHORPE
St. Michael and All Angels: John Maunsell Richardson, Ann Smith

EVINGTON
St. Denys: James Sherard

EXTON
St. Peter and St. Paul: Baptist Noel – 3rd Viscount Campden

FROLESWORTH
St. Nicholas: John Smith

GADDESBY
St. Luke: Colonel Edward Cheney

GLENFIELD
St. Peter (Old Church): Thomas Hassall

HALLATON
St. Michael and All Angels: Reverend George Fenwicke

HAMBLETON
St. Andrew: Amelia Woodcock

HATHERN
St. Peter and St. Paul: Reverend Andrew Glen

HIGHAM-ON-THE-HILL
St. Peter: Fisher Family

HINCKLEY
St. Mary: William Burton, Dr Robert Chessher, Joseph Nutt, Richard Smith

HUSBANDS BOSWORTH
All Saints: John Shenton, Henry Smith

KETTON
St. Mary: William Hibbins

KIBWORTH
St. Wilfrid: Roger Deacon, Michael Ingo, Lewis Powel Williams

KING'S NORTON
St. John the Baptist: Fortrey Family

KIRBY MUXLOE
St. Bartholomew: Samuel Adcock

KIRKBY MALLORY
All Saints: Augusta Ada King – Countess of Lovelace

KNIGHTON
St. Mary Magdalene: Annie Elizabeth Greatorex, Denzil Jarvis

LAUGHTON
St. Luke: Colonel Wiliam Cole, Reverend William Cave Humfrey

LEICESTER
King Lear, King Richard III
All Saints: Alderman Gabriel Newton
County Gaol (now Leicester Prison): William Brown
Gilroes Cemetery: Tommy (Henry Ernest) Atkins, Walter Bates, Wiliam H. Friswell, Sir Mark Henig, Bennett Southwell
Leicester Abbey: Cardinal Thomas Wolsey
The Newarke: Mary de Bohun, Earls of Leicester
Saffron Lane – Aylestone Road: James Cook
St. Leonard: James Cook
St. Margaret: Mary Linwood
St. Martin: James Andrewe, John Fenton, Sir William Herrick, John Johnson, King Richard III, Joseph Smith, Abigail Swift, Dr William Watts
St. Mary de Castro: Baron Lawrence Carter, Reverend William Ludlam
Welford Road Cemetery: John Biggs, Amos Booth, Thomas Cook, Joseph Dare, John Ellis, John Flower, William Gardiner, Joseph Gordon, Bert (Albert Walter) Harris, William (Jack) Joyce, Ted (Edwin) Meadows, Arthur Dick Pougher, John William Stephens, Clement Stretton

LOCKINGTON-CUM-HEMINGTON
St. Nicholas: Reverend Robert Laycock Story

LONG WHATTON
All Saints: Aaron Boswell

LOUGHBOROUGH
All Saints: Thomas Bombrosse, Loughborough Tradespeople, William Peck, William Smith
Emmanuel: Robert Burnaby
Old Rectory Museum: Sarah Johnson
Woodgate Baptist Church: Sarah Johnson

LUBENHAM
St. Mary: Christopher Risley Perkins

LUTTERWORTH
St. Mary: William Banbury, John Wycliffe

LYNDON
St. Martin: Thomas Barker, William Whiston

MARKET BOSWORTH
St. Peter: Robert Pull

MARKET HARBOROUGH
St. Mary in Arden: Samuel Rouse, Samuel Turner

MEDBOURNE
St. Giles: Dr William Watts

MELTON MOWBRAY
St. Mary: Sir John Digby, John Ferneley, Sir Francis Grant
St. Mary's Close C. of E. Cemetery: Sir Francis Grant

MOUNT ST. BERNARD ABBEY
Anselm Baker

MUSTON
St. John the Baptist: Sarah Crabbe

NAILSTONE
All Saints: Thomas Corbett

NEWTON HARCOURT
St. Luke: Christopher Gardner, Sir Henry St. John Halford

NEWTOWN LINFORD
All Saints: ABCD Tombstone

NORMANTON
St. Matthew: Sir Gilbert Heathcote

NORTH LUFFENHAM
St. John the Baptist: Archdeacon Robert Johnson, Vincent Wing

NOSELEY
St. Mary's Chapel: Sir Arthur Hesilrige

OADBY
Oadby Cemetery: Jimmy (James) Hawker

OLD DALBY
St. John the Baptist: Edward Purdey

PECKLETON
St. Mary Magdalene: Thomas Boothby, Chataway Family, Dr Robert Chessher, Taft Family

PRESTWOLD
St. Andrew: Sir Christopher Packe

QUORN
St. Bartholomew: John Farnham, Tom Firr

REDMILE
St. Peter: Reverend Thomas Daffy

ROTHLEY
St. Mary and St. John the Baptist: Sampson Cartwright

SALTBY
King Lud

SAPCOTE
All Saints: Thomas Ball

SAXELBYE
St. Peter: Esther Houghton

SCRAPTOFT
All Saints: James Wigley

SHEARSBY
St. Mary Magdalene: Wiliam Weston

SHEPSHED
St. Botolph: Giovanni Modena, Thomas Wean

SILEBY
St. Mary: Edward Baradell

SLAWSTON
All Saints: Wilfred Bollard, Samuel Granger

SOUTH KILWORTH
St. Nicholas: William Clark, Reverend William Pearson

SOUTH LUFFENHAM
St. Mary: Rose Boswell

STAPLEFORD
St. Mary Magdalene: Geoffrey Sherard

STATHERN
St. Guthlac: Thomas Bugg, Colonel Francis Hacker

STAUNTON HAROLD
Holy Trinity: Laurence Shirley – 4th Earl Ferrers

STOCKERSTON
St. Peter: Sir Thomas Burton

STOKE GOLDING
St. Margaret: Henry Firebrace

STONEY STANTON
St. Michael: Reverend John Bold, John Orton

STOUGHTON
St. Mary and All Saints: Thomas Farnham, Annie Bella Wright

SUTTON CHENEY
St. James: King Richard III, Thomas Simpson

SWEPSTONE
William Lole

SWITHLAND
St. Leonard: Sir John Danvers, Sir Joseph Danvers

TEIGH
Holy Trinity: Anthony Jenkinson

THEDDINGWORTH
All Saints: George Bathurst

THRINGSTONE
St. Andrew: Charles Booth

THRUSSINGTON
Holy Trinity: John Ferneley

THURCASTON
All Saints: Elias Travers

THURNBY
St. Luke: Charles Bennion

TWYFORD
St. Andrew: Thomas Holland, Absalom Smith

UPPINGHAM
St. Peter and St. Paul: Edward Thring

WANLIP
Our Lady and St. Nicholas: Rasselas Morjan

WELHAM
St. Andrew: Edwards Family

WHITWICK
Whitwick Cemetery: Thomas Ashford

WIGSTON
All Saints: George Davenport
Wigston Cemetery: Gertie Gitana (Gertrude Ross), Don Ross

WILLOUGHBY WATERLEYS
St. Mary: Thomas Hill

WISTOW
St. Wistan: Sir Henry Halford, Sir Henry St. John Halford, Sir Richard Halford

WOODHOUSE
St. Mary in the Elms: William Beston

WYMONDHAM
St. Peter: Sir Thomas Berkeley, Helen Hayes, Joseph Hayes, Samuel Pears

Leicestershire churches which have particularly fine collections of interior monuments include:

Ashby-de-la-Zouch: St. Helen (Hastings)
Bottesford: St. Mary (Manners)
Breedon-on-the-Hill: St. Mary and St. Hardulph (Shirley)
Exton: St. Peter and St. Paul (Harington, Noel)
Fenny Drayton: St, Michael and All Angels (Purefoy)
Kirkby Mallory: All Saints (Noel)
Leicester: St. Martin (various)
Lockington-cum-Hemington: St. Nicholas (Bainbrigge)
Market Bosworth: St. Peter (Dixie)
Noseley: St. Mary's Chapel (Hesilrige)
Old Dalby: St. John the Baptist (Noel)
Prestwold: St. Andrew (Packe, Skipworth)
Quorn: St. Bartholomew (Farnham)
Shepshed: St. Botolph (Phillipps)
Stapleford: St. Mary Magdalene (Sherard)
Stoke Dry: St. Andrew (Digby)
Thurlaston: All Saints (Turville)
Tilton-on-the-Hill: St. Peter (Digby)
Wistow: St. Wistan (Halford)

(The principal family or families commemorated are in brackets)

Detail from William Bainbrigge's outstanding highly coloured wall monument, St. Nicholas Lockington-cum-Hemington

Of the great many Leicestershire churchyards and burial grounds which have interesting collections of tombstones, the following are a short personal selection:

Ab Kettleby: St. James; Ashwell: St. Mary; Barton-in-the-Beans: General Baptist Chapel; Burton Lazars: St. James; Gaddesby: St. Luke; Great Casterton: St. Peter and St. Paul; Hinckley: St. Mary; Ketton: St. Mary; Kirby Muxloe: St. Bartholomew; Leicester: Great Meeting; Leicester: St. Margaret; Leicester: St. Mary de Castro; Leicester: Welford Road Cemetery; Long Clawson: St. Remigias; Loughborough: All Saints; Market Harborough: St. Mary in Arden; Newton Harcourt: St. Luke; Rothley: St. Mary and St. John the Baptist; Swithland: St. Leonard.

Ketton churchyard which has many fine examples of the stonemasons' art

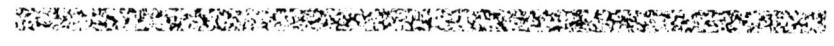

Index to people

(M) Signifies a monument, memorial or gravestone is still known to exist in a Leicestershire church, churchyard, cemetery or other burial ground.
For further information, see the relevant entry.

To see at a glance who is associated with where, consult the **Gazetteer.**

Adams, Rev James Williams (M)   107-9
Adcock, Samuel (M)   128
Andrewe, James (M)   11-2
Anon. ABCD Tombstone (M)   25-6
Ashford, Thomas   107-9
Atkins, Tommy (Henry Ernest)   113
Baker, Anselm (M)   68
Bakewell, Robert (M)   46-7
Ball, Thomas (M)   177
Banbury, William (M)   118
Baradell, Edward (M)   167-8
Barker, Thomas (M)   48-9
Barsby, Henry (M)   133
Bates, Walter (M)   178
Bathurst, George (M)   156
Beaumont, Sir George Howland (M)   59-60
Bennion, Charles (M)   98-9
Berkeley, Sir Thomas (M)   148
Beston, William (M)   140
Biggs, John (M)   90-1
Biggs, William (M)   90
Bohun, Mary de   144
Bold, Rev John (M)   82-3
Bollard, Wilfred (M)   116
Bombrosse, Thomas (M)   132-3
Booth, Amos (M)   97-8
Booth, Charles (M)   96-7
Boothby, Thomas (M)   101-2
Boswell, Aaron   28-9
Boswell, Rose (M)   28-30
Brown, William   129
Bugg, Thomas   70
Bullen, Rev Edward (M)   102-3

Burnaby, Robert (M)   185
Burton, Sir Thomas (M)   179
Burton, William (M)   168-9
Carter, Baron Lawrence (M)   164-5
Cartwright, Sampson   72
Cave, Joseph (M)   76
Cave, Theophilus (M)   13-4
Chataway Family (M)   186-7
Cheney, Colonel Edward (M)   30-1
Chessher, Dr Robert (M)   52
Clark, Nathaniel (M)   136-7
Clark, William (M)   172
Clayton, "Uncle" Edward Chapman (M)   112
Cole, Colonel William (M)   161
Cook, James   126-8
Cook, Thomas (M)   94-6
Cooper, Lady Diana   116-7
Corbett, Thomas (M)   151-2
Crabbe, Sarah (M)   181-2
Crossley, John Sydney (M)   56-7
Crozier, Temple (M)   137-8
Daffy, Rev Thomas   36-7
Danvers, Sir John (M)   70-1
Danvers, Sir Joseph (M)   18-9
Dare, Joseph (M)   91-3
Davenport, George   124-5
Deacon, Roger (M)   137
Deacon, Samuel (M)   51
Digby, Sir John   148-9
Edwards Family (M)   20-1
Ellis, John (M)   88-9
Farnham, John (M)   151
Farnham, Thomas (M)   151

209

Fenton, John (M)   122-3
Fenwicke, Rev George (M)   22
Fenwicke, Rev William (M)   22
Ferneley, John (M)   63-4
Firebrace, Henry (M)   160
Firr, Tom (M)   106-7
Fisher Family (M)   186
Flower, John (M)   65-6
Fortrey Family (M)   21-2
Friswell, William H.   78-9
Gardiner, William (M)   62-3
Gardner, Christopher (M)   34
Gitana, Gertie (M)   114-5
Glen, Rev Andrew   38
Gordon, Joseph (M)   57-8
Granger, Samuel (M)   135
Grant, Sir Francis (M)   66-7
Greatorex, Annie Elizabeth   182
Greene, Sir Raymond (M)   187
Hacker, Colonel Francis   159
Halford, Sir Henry (M)   53-4
Halford, Sir Henry St. John (M)   105
Halford, Sir Richard (M)   156-7
Hanbury, Rev William (M)   84-5
Harris, Bert (Albert Walter) (M)   103-4
Hassall, Thomas (M)   177
Hastings, Ferdinando   11-2
Hastings, Selina, Countess of Huntingdon (M)   86-7
Hawker, Jimmy (James) (M)   77-8
Hayes, Helen (M)   33
Hayes, Joseph (M)   33
Hazlerigg see Hesilrige
Heathcote, Sir Gilbert (M)   162-4
Henig, Sir Mark (M)   99-100
Herrick, Abigail see Swift, Abigail
Herrick, Sir William (M)   154-5
Hesilrige, Sir Arthur (M)   157-8
Heyricke see Herrick
Hibbins, William (M)   169-70
Hill, Thomas (M)   135
Holland, Thomas (M)   171
Houghton, Esther (M)   27
Humfrey, Rev William Cave (M)   102
Ingo, Michael (M)   137
Jarvis, Denzil (M)   140
Jenkinson, Anthony   153

John, King   142
Johnson, John (1) (M)   49-50
Johnson, John (2) (M)   121-2
Johnson, Archdeacon Robert (M)   81-2
Johnson, Sarah (M)   27-8
Joyce, William (Jack) (M)   139
King, Augusta Ada, Countess of Lovelace (M)   183-4
Kirkland, Dr Thomas (M)   48
Kitchener, Colonel Henry Horatio (M)   185-6
Lancaster, Henry 1st Duke of   144
Lancaster, Henry Earl of   144
Lear, King   141
Leicester, Earls of   144
Linwood, Mary (M)   61-2
Lole, William   73-4
Loughborough Tradespeople (M)   167
Lud, King   141-2
Ludlam, Rev William   45
Mammatt, Edward (M)   65
Manners, Francis, 6th Earl of Rutland (M)   9-11
Manners, John, Marquis of Granby   165-6
Marvin, Samuel   171-2
Massey, John   125-6
Meadows, Ted (Edwin) (M)   139
Michel, Rev Humfrey   69-70
Modena, Giovanni (M)   176
Morjan, Rasselas (M)   175-6
Newton, Alderman Gabriel (M)   83-4
Noel, Baptist, 3rd Viscount Campden (M)   15-6
Nutt, Joseph (M)   43
Orton, John (M)   168
Packe, Sir Christopher (M)   162-3
Parsons, Richard (M)   118-9
Pears, Samuel (M)   173
Pearson, Rev William (M)   54-5
Peck, William (M)   132-3
Perkins, Christopher Risley (M)   79
Pougher, Arthur Dick   111
Powell, Mary (M)   181
Prior, John (M)   48
Pull, Robert (M)   39
Purdey, Edward (M)   120
Richard III, King (M)   144-7
Richardson, John Maunsell (M)   110
Roberts, Sir Richard (M)   153-4
Roos, Robert de (M)   143

Ross, Don (M)   114-5
Ross, Gertrude see Gitana, Gertie
Rouse, Samuel   42
Shenton, John (M)   161
Sherard, Geoffrey (M)   148-9
Sherard, James (M)   38-9
Shirley, Laurence, 4th Earl Ferrers   121-2
Simpson, Thomas (M)   40-1
Smith, Absalom   28-30
Smith, Ann (M)   11
Smith, Henry   101
Smith, John (M)   162
Smith, Joseph (M)   174
Smith, Richard (M)   119-20
Smith, William (M)   132-3
Southwell, Bennett (M)   112-3
Squire, William (M)   24-5
Stavelie, Thomas (M)   12
Stephens, John William   74-6
Stokes, Rev Edward (M)   87-8
Story, Rev Robert Laycock   105-6
Stretton, Clement (M)   58
Swann, Robert (M)   17
Swift, Abigail   180
Taft Family   186-7
Taylor, Joseph (M)   133
Thring, Edward (M)   93
Travers, Elias (M)   13
Turner, Samuel (M)   169-70
Turner, William (M)   183
Twining, Mary see Powell, Mary
Twining, Richard (M)   32
Vaughan see Halford
Watts, Dr William (M)   43-4
Wean, Thomas (M)   136
Webb, Morpeth (M)   35
Weston, William (M)   134
Whiston, William (M)   39-40
Wigley, James (M)   22-3
Williams, Lewis Powel (M)   41-2
Wing, Vincent   36
Wolsey, Cardinal Thomas (M)   149-50
Woodcock, Amelia (M)   55-6
Wright, Annie Bella (M)   130-1
Wycliffe, John (M)   80-1
Zborowski, Count Luigi (M)   110-1
Zborowski, Count William Elliott (M)   110-1